What to do

When
Your
Dreams
Don't
Come True

What to do

When
Your
Dreams
Don't
Come True

by
David Shibley

New Leaf Press

New Leaf Edition
1993

Library of Congress Catalog No. 92-63374
ISBN: 0-89221-232-2

Scripture quotations, unless otherwise indicated, are from the *New King James Version of the Holy Bible* copyright © 1979, 1980, 1982 by Thomas Nelson Publishers. Italics throughout have been added by the author.

Cover Photo: J & J Tiner Photographs

This book was originally titled *Dreams Lost and Found*.

CONTENTS

Author's Preface 7

1. The Stuff Dreams Are Made Of 11

2. Life's Detours 29

3. An Appointed Time 53

4. The Fine Art of Forgiveness 67

5. Recovering the Cutting Edge 77

6. The Vision Refocused 95

7. When It Can't Be Fixed 105

8. Your Alabaster Box 115

9. The College of Disappointments 121

10. The Sanctity of Brokenness 129

11. Leave a Well 145

12. Can These Bones Live? 157

13. A Fresh Cluster of Promise 167

For

wounded

dreamers

Author's Preface

We are at the changing of the guard. The postwar leaders of the Church are fast passing from the scene. The recent deaths of several of these pioneers signal the ending of an era.

Now, more than ever, there is a screaming need for capable leadership in Christian circles. Today's emerging leaders must be more concerned with integrity than stage presence. They must mix compassion and sensitivity with global vision.

But there's a problem. Where are these upcoming leaders? Too often, they simply aren't available. Many of the most promising have opted out of the battle because of discouragement. Their budding ambition was crushed by some disappointment. Thus the Church has been left almost bereft of one of its most precious assets: Spirit-anointed, biblically oriented leaders.

Scandals and startling revelations have rocked the Christian world. Charges and counter-charges have flown like missiles through the Church, leaving the body of Christ confused, fractured, and wounded. Our corporate crisis is augmented by the personal crises of many individual believers who are struggling to regain their spiritual equilibrium and personal dignity. As all of this occurs, anti-Christians have a heyday at our expense.

Yet at the same time dramatically wonderful things are happening. The honor of the name of Christ is being restored. The gospel is advancing with unprecedented speed. We are on the brink of the greatest breakthroughs toward world evangelization in history. The Church is marching!

But, we are also stalling. While much is being said about conquest, the truth is that we must move cautiously in order to care for the vast number of debilitated soldiers. Everywhere I go I see them, strewn in the gutters along life's path. Once impassioned dreamers now lie bleeding and immobilized.

Many are like the crippled man at the pool of Bethesda. While he clung to faint optimism, much of his life had been spent in brokenness and waiting. He had just enough desire to keep showing up, morning after morning, in the distant hope that the next miracle might be his. Yet he was so demoralized that he had consigned all his hopes to merely human intervention: "I have no man."

Just so, many today are dolefully hoping to be in just the right place to get just the right break from just the right person to launch their dreams into reality. But when Jesus passes by, breaks are no longer necessary. All that is needed is His touch on their crippled condition, His command to rise and walk.

However, Jesus is no broad-brush magician. He releases His healing only on those who truly desire it. "Do you *want* to be whole?" was the question on which all of this crippled man's future hinged. Today, Jesus asks you the same question. He's passing your way, not to toss you into some pool of chance, but to bring fresh life to your brokenness by His Word.

You may be one of life's wounded. If so, this book is for you. Hundreds of hours have been invested in prayer, writing, and editing. If the Church is to recover its dream of glory, you must recover yours. And whether your longing is for restored usefulness, a restored hope, or a restored future, your dream can live again. Once again, you can know heaven's touch on your pent-up hopes.

— David Shibley

1

The Stuff Dreams Are Made Of

*For I know the thoughts that I think toward you,
says the Lord, thoughts of peace and not of evil, to give
you a future and a hope (Jer. 29:11).*

Man, I was going to change the world," Bob half-laughed as he shook his head. He took another sip of coffee and I saw a dash of anger fill his eyes. "Do you know what I really can't understand?" he said. "I thought the Lord put those dreams in my heart. Now it doesn't look like they will ever come true. Those dreams gave me a reason to keep going. Why should I keep going now?" Bob, like so many, was trying to come to grips with unfulfilled dreams.

Jan stopped me at the front of our church after I had preached on establishing a Christian home. "Please pray for us, David." She brushed back the tears. "When Bill and I were engaged I read every book on Christian marriage I could find. But now we're in the middle of an ugly divorce. There doesn't seem to be any hope of reconciliation." Another shattered dream.

"I really thought we had faith for Timmy's healing." Carol seemed to be retracing painful memories as we sat in my office. "We seemed to have so many assurances that he would get well. But when he died . . . ." her voice cracked. She didn't need to say any more. The grief and confusion screamed what words couldn't say.

Then there was Jim. He had embarked on a business venture for the sole purpose of assisting Christian ministries. He had structured the company so that all profit went directly to the Lord's work. But there was no profit. Instead, Jim was faced with lawsuits from angry creditors.

The world is filled with people who must cope with unfulfilled hopes. Perhaps that is why you picked up this book. What can you do when your dreams don't come true? Can you recover lost hopes? Can you risk nurturing new hopes?

This is a book about motivation and motives, about success and failure, about realized aspirations and dreams that never came true. It's about recovering lost perspective and daring to hope again, even after bitter disappointment.

"We are such stuff as dreams are made on,"[1] said Shakespeare. We thrive on desires and aspirations. They are second nature to us. Before infants can talk they attempt to express their wishes — their hopes for something better or for something more.

Children quickly learn that dreams also lace their parents' thoughts. "Daddy, what color is our ship?" a preschool girl asked.

"Sweetheart, we don't have any ship," her father laughed.

"Yes we do, Daddy," the little girl retorted. "You're always talking about when our ship comes in!"

And so we are. These longings for something better or for something more (or if we're dieting, something less!) drive us, encourage us, and often come back to haunt us. For all too soon life's realities teach us that the road to something more is barricaded. And if we look in the rearview mirror we quickly see discarded dreams and dashed hopes strewn along our path.

To a greater or lesser degree disappointment is one of the most common of human occurrences, perhaps ranking only behind the universal experiences of birth and death. Winston Churchill echoed the sentiments of much of humankind when he said, "We are so often mocked by the failure of our hopes."[2] And that statement is from a man most people would consider an eminent success.

Life is comprised of both successes and failures. And the failure ledger often seems much thicker than the record of success. Yet, tragically, when scarred people with unfulfilled dreams turn to the Church for guidance and fresh hope, too frequently they find that the Church has only a theology for success. We hesitate to address the subject of failure. Yet it is one of the most common human experiences.

And the experience of failure is not always bad. Often we don't stop to realize that failure can be the back door to success. Thomas Edison's inventions were almost always the result of trial and error. Abraham Lincoln came back from a landslide defeat to be elected president. Charles DeGaulle was "finished" in the 1940s, only to emerge as France's great post-war leader. Catherine Marshall overcame stinging grief and showed thousands of others how they could live again through her inspirational writings.

Yes, it is certainly possible to experience triumph after tragedy. But this is not always clear to us when we are in the midst of tragedy. When dreams die, energy to dream for the future often dies as well.

Ambition: Oxygen for the Spirit

Dreams are oxygen for the spirit. Hope pumps life into the inner person. Ambition is a kind of emotional adrenaline that keeps us aspiring to better and greater achievement.

Yet even speaking in terms of achievement may need clarification in our day. We live in a secularized world powered by ambitious people. To a large degree, driven people steer the course of events. Consequently, Christians have often responded to secularized ambition in extremes. We tend either to baptize all ambition or to bury it.

For example, much Christian teaching today seems to be little more than positivism plastered with religious jargon. While the gospel is unquestionably positive and the most wonderful Good News in the world, we do violence to the Scriptures if we never address the issues of sorrow, loss, suffering, and failure.

At the same time, a macabre, constant emphasis on a flagellating self-denial is also imbalanced. We so often make issues *either/or* that should be *both/and*. The biblical message is not one of triumph versus tragedy, one or the other. Rather, it is a message of triumph *over* tragedy.

There is a desperate need today to strike a balance. On the one hand we must stop punishing ourselves for sins Jesus has already borne for us. We must quit playing games of "evangelical penance."

On the other hand, we cannot kid ourselves into thinking that a good attitude about life is the heart of the Christian message. The clear teaching of Scripture is that we are sinners in need of a Saviour. We must cease preaching "faith in faith" and recover our distinctive of faith in Christ and His atoning work. It's too late in the game to appeal to a "hope in hope." Rather we must obey the scriptural injunction to hope in the Lord who made heaven and earth.

Ambition is amoral. In itself ambition is neither moral nor immoral. It is only polluted by wrong thinking, greed, and purely material responses to life's stimuli. The way we use ambition either stains it or makes it noble. Ambition can spur a physically challenged person to become an artist against all odds. Or it can turn a petty thief into an arch-criminal.

So the question is not whether ambition is good or bad. The question is whether or not the dreams behind our ambition are born of God. Desires may have their origins in heaven, hell, or our own minds. We need discernment to know the source of our dreams.

God himself plants many dreams in our hearts. They are implanted as seeds to be fertilized by ambition. God is not in the business of playing teasing, chase-but-never-catch games with His children. He does not put a carrot on a stick, permanently out of reach of the exhausted aspirant. God is not some cruel master who beckons us to jump like dogs, only to lift the thing desired barely above our highest efforts.

If a dream has been put into your heart by God, He has placed it there for eventual fulfillment. But as we move toward the realization of our dreams, God will allow stops along the way for attitude checkups. If we don't like what we see, we may tend to zoom past the next warning light that signals us to stop for our next checkup on motives.

True, all dreams that are God-birthed bring blessing to us, but the accomplishment of these dreams is also meant to bring glory to God. It is possible to begin the race with pure motives and end with bad ones. What may have been birthed for His honor can quickly degenerate into a lustful drive for personal accolades.

Acceptance and approval are, of course, basic human needs. We all need affirmation. It is when these needs become primary, more important to us than glorifying God, that these legitimate needs become sordid. Check your motives. Is your dream birthed in heaven or from a subliminal need to materially or even spiritually "keep up with the Joneses?"

Realizing Your Dreams

Alexander Pope wrote, "Hope springs eternal in the human breast."[3] Even after crushing disappointments, most people have the capacity to get up, dust themselves off emotionally, and begin again. We function as goal-oriented people, even if we do not articulate the goals. The peasant in a Third World country has a goal of carrying water from the well to the village. The corporate executive may have goals of a far different kind, but we all have goals. Goals are interrelated with needs. When we advance to the place that our primal needs are met, then our goals are no longer survival-oriented but fulfillment- and purpose-oriented.

Through the prophet Joel, God promised that one of the telltale signs of the latter days would be a renewal of spiritual dreams and visions. "And it shall come to pass afterward that I will pour out My Spirit on all flesh; your sons and your daughters shall prophesy, your old men shall dream dreams, your young men shall see visions; and also on My menservants and on My maidservants I will pour out My Spirit in those days" (Joel 2:28-29). We are living in such a time. The boldest and most far-flung endeavors in the history of Christianity are being undertaken in our day. God is opening up the hearts and minds of young and old alike to see beyond former boundaries.

I'll never forget as a young preacher sharing some of my hopes with a Christian sculptor and pottery-maker. His name was John Frank. His Frankoma Pottery had been donated to hundreds of churches over the years. I had watched him write out checks for thousands of dollars to Christian ministries. Often he would literally laugh as he wrote the checks. He was definitely a "cheerful giver." He possessed the spiritual gift of giving. Though he is now home with the Lord, his designer plates and pottery bear ample worldwide evidence of his joyful creativity.

He used his wealth to advance the cause of Christ.

And he had a good deal of wealth to share. What most people don't know is that John Frank went broke several times before his pottery business finally took off. He knew much about how the Master Potter can, at His discretion, remake or even break trial molds of clay until He produces His masterpiece.

John Frank gave me two great bits of advice. "First," he said, "never be late in making a payment." Then he looked at me intently. "Second, always dream big dreams. It doesn't cost any more to dream big dreams than it does to dream little ones. And you'll never realize a dream you haven't had."

So if your trial shapes and model clay pots have been discarded or even dashed against an unrelenting wall of reality, dream again. Remember John Frank's advice: You'll never realize a dream you haven't had.

Your Elusive Dream

Granted, it's not always easy to bounce back after your hopes have been shattered. But remember, if you're discouraged, you're in no frame of mind to make life-altering decisions. It is difficult, if not impossible, to be objective about your future when you're still smarting from a past disappointment. Your hopes may seem evasive, but determine to keep dreaming.

A small plaque hangs in my study. I remember that it hung in my grandparents' kitchen when I was a small boy. Each time I pass it, I read its words again. I know very little about its author, Ella Wheeler Wilcox, but I am certain she was no stranger to the batterings of life. That poet understood that, more often than not, dreams are realized by knowing precisely where you are headed and by being willing to keep set in that direction.

One ship goes east, another west,
by the self-same winds that blow.
'Tis the set of the sail and not the gale,
that determines the way they go.

Like the ships at sea are the ways of man
as we voyage along through life.
'Tis the set of the soul that decides the goal,
and not the calm or strife.[4]

The "set of the soul" does indeed determine our destiny. Our eternal destination is determined by a "set of the soul" to follow Jesus Christ in a commitment to Him as Saviour and Lord. Our temporal destiny — what our lives will accomplish on earth — is also determined by the "set of our sail," and not the gales that blow in a contrary fashion.

Vince Lombardi was one of the greatest coaches in the history of professional football. He led his Green Bay Packers from humiliating defeats to world championships in the 1960s. Coach Lombardi said, "The greatest success is not in never falling but in rising every time you fall."

Most of the time we are not allowed to choose whether or not we will be dealt severe blows in life. What we can choose is whether we will stay down for the count or get up — and keep getting up — again.

You may feel that you are down for the count; now you must choose. You can throw in the towel. Or you can get up again. But you — and only you — can make the choice.

I realize that most people who pick up a book like this have battled with adversity. You haven't opened this book by accident. God has a message for you. You can get up. You can dream again. There is a future for you. Those hidden aspirations are the stuff dreams are made of.

> *You haven't opened this book by accident. God has a message for you. You can get up. You can dream again. There is a future for you.*

It's time for you to get up, dust yourself off, and dream again. God's creativity is constant yet new to us every day.

Heaven is transmitting dreams to us all the time — if only we have ears to hear, eyes to see, hearts to dream.

Reassessing Your Dreams: The Midlife Crisis

Much has been written about the trauma of midlife crisis. Such an experience is not unique to men. Women, as well, often wake up one morning and ask, "Is this all there is? Is this all my life is going to accomplish? Have I realized what I wanted — much less what God wanted — through my life?"

True success in life is simply to know the will of God and do it. Of course, the general will of God for every Christian is to glorify God all the days of one's life in joyful obedience. But the specific will of God, that unique "something" that God can accomplish only through you, is the true measure of your life's success. Paul, approaching impending martyrdom, was able to tell Timothy, "I have fought the good fight, I have finished the race, I have kept the faith" (2 Tim. 4:7). In essence he was saying, "I have accomplished God's will for my life."

What is the specialized "something" you are to do, that unique accomplishment that can only come through you? Think back to the dream that used to drive you. How are you progressing toward seeing it fulfilled?

The midlife crisis in a believer's life is often a reassessment of his or her progress toward accomplishing God's unique purpose. And as we assess our accomplishments and, more noticeably, our lack of them, we must meet head-on the issue of unfulfilled dreams. Some years ago I faced a midlife crisis. After reaching the "halfway point" of thirty-five, I asked the Holy Spirit to examine my heart, my motives, my accomplishments, and my discarded hopes. As the Spirit spotlighted my life, I didn't like everything I saw. Some crevasses, long darkened by time, contained both joy and pain.

When the Lord called me to preach at age sixteen, I remember making two very specific requests. "Number one, Lord, make my life significant in Your cause. And, number two, take me home to heaven before I would ever bring major dishonor to the gospel."

That is still my heart's prayer today. God has graciously used me as one of His instruments. I have had privileges that few have in a lifetime. I've preached in over thirty nations. Thousands have come to Christ. I've preached in many of the world's greatest churches.

But there are also dreams that have been lost. I remembered, for instance, all of the books God put into my heart that were never written. More than once I've walked through a bookstore and seen "my" book. God had given me clear vision for it two or three years previously. I just never responded. Or I didn't respond in time. The seasonal door of opportunity was now shut. I reminisced over other lost opportunities. Television programs that were never produced. Gospel broadcasts that I once produced but are now tapes getting brittle in my attic.

And on a personal level, I thought about our little girl who never came. Although Naomi and I have two terrific sons whom we love with all our hearts, the daughter was not to be. Then I thought of Naomi's miscarriage at a traumatic time when we were leaving a pastorate in Arkansas to go to seminary in Texas. Was that our little girl?

And what of the other unfulfilled hopes? So many "unfinished symphonies" premiered only before God, Naomi, and me. What do you do when your dreams don't come true? And how could I help others deal with their broken hopes?

Retrievable or Irretrievable?

Thankfully, I'm on the other side of that season of introspection. At present, I'm not plagued with any strong regret over unfulfilled dreams. In fact, I seem to be swimming in opportunities — seeking strength to seize the new ideas and possibilities and wisdom to prioritize all that the Lord is putting in my heart.

This opportunity of viewing the subject of dreams at arm's length helped me see that the road to recovery from unrealized aspirations is first of all to isolate what *kind* of dreams were unfulfilled. Our unfulfilled aspirations fall into two distinct categories: retrievable dreams and irretrievable dreams. That unfulfilled dream in your heart, is it a retrievable dream or an irretrievable one? By that I mean, is there any possibility that it still *could* happen?

For instance, I have a friend in a wheelchair. We both believe in the power of God to heal her and enable her to walk again. We have prayed and believed for several years for her healing. I know she can be healed. I have seen people get up out of wheelchairs during crusades where I have preached overseas. But, as yet, she cannot walk.

Can she be healed? Is it possible? The answer is yes. Her dream of walking can be realized. In the meantime she must cope with how to live productively until her miracle happens — if it happens.

You may wonder, "Although it may be possible that she will be healed, is it probable?" We cannot know. Some things are simply in the hands of a sovereign God. Very often life is more complex than the pre-cut responses of our theology or our level of faith. On the one hand, we are not to be faithless. On the other hand, we yield to God's ultimate sovereignty.

Jason has a retrievable dream as well. He has dreamed for years of being financially independent. He also wants freedom of time so that he can give large amounts of both time and money to overseas team missions endeavors. He's taken a couple of cracks at it. His marketing business was great — for a few months. Then it folded. His retail store was unsuccessful, too. Presently, he keeps office hours and draws a relatively small salary in somebody else's company. He feels that he's advancing that company's dream but not his own.

Does this mean that Jason's dream of financial independence is unattainable? That his dream is irretrievable? No. Admittedly there are roadblocks to the realization of his hopes, but such a dream can still come true. Jason, like my friend in the wheelchair, must live in the healthy tension of being presently happy and productive while not letting his vision dim.

Elaine, however, must deal with her unrealized dream differently. She had hoped and prayed for her mother's recovery, but her mother died on the operating table. Now Elaine must come to grips with the reality of the loss. Just as she gave her mother's body a proper burial, now she must give her hopes concerning her mother a proper burial as well. Certainly this does not mean that her mother and memories of her will ever cease to be precious to her, but it does mean that Elaine cannot allow these memories, precious though they are, to blind her to present realities or restrict her from present happiness. Elaine must acknowledge that the dream of her mother's recovery is irretrievable.

Cindi, too, must acknowledge that her dream cannot be realized. She had held on for the reconciliation of her marriage. She continued to fight for the preservation of her family even when her husband's infidelity was undeniable. Even after the divorce (which she contested) was finalized, she still prayed for eventual remarriage and healing of the home.

It didn't happen. Her husband promptly married the other woman. Now Cindi, like Elaine, must lay her dream to rest. She cannot, as some have ludicrously suggested, wish harm or even death on her former husband's new wife, hoping that would bring him back to her. To desire such a calamity on anyone, even on someone who has hurt us, is violently opposed to Christian ethics and is clearly a violation of the biblical injunction to absolve those who have wronged us. Jesus taught us, "Love your enemies, bless those who curse you, do good to those who hate you, and pray for those who spitefully use you and persecute you" (Matt. 5:44). She must lay that dream to rest.

So, you see, your response to broken dreams must be determined by what kind of dreams they are. Is your unfulfilled dream retrievable? Then fan the dimly burning flame. God does not wish to break your hope (or you) beyond repair. "A bruised reed He will not break, and smoking flax He will not quench" (Isa. 42:3). So keep on dreaming. Your retrievable dream can still come true.

If, however, you have suffered more than a temporary setback your dream may indeed be irretrievable. In that case, do two things. First, acknowledge it. Your road back to emotional recovery is to live in reality, understanding that your cherished hope will not be realized. Second, don't despair. Only when you lay your irretrievable dream to rest can you dare to dream again.

When Dreams Do Come True

Someone has caustically remarked that the only thing worse than unrealized dreams is realized ones. This can indeed be true if we take the short cut to achievement. The road to lasting success is almost never the path of least resistance. Such success is usually short-lived.

We are living in an integrity crisis. It is an enigmatic time when gargantuan dreams are indeed being realized. But too often there is not the underpinning of personal character to support the empire that has emerged. No one questions the pain of living with dreams that never came true. Perhaps it is an even greater pain, however, to watch a realized dream crumble because it had an inadequate support system.

Since 1987 we have witnessed the rise and fall of several Christian enterprises and the people behind them. This is always agonizing and tragic, not only for those who are directly involved but also for the larger Christian community who are scripturally enjoined to bear each other's burdens. "Brethren, if a man is overtaken in any trespass, you who are spiritual restore such a one in a spirit of gentleness, considering yourself lest you also be tempted. Bear one another's burdens [sorrows], and so fulfill the law of Christ" (Gal. 6:1-2).

It is often frightening to watch someone with passionate ambition claw his way to the top, even in a Christian endeavor. For a person who is driven only by the goal of success will usually be oblivious to the people he leaves in the dust along the way. By the time he gets to the top, he may have adopted a flawed work ethic that sees people as expendable commodities. He begins to think only in quantum terms. Thus, this aggressive leader may have a great compassion for "humanity" but little or no concern for the actual persons that mass of people comprises.

Of course, such an empire is built on a very tenuous foundation. Persons always make or break any organization or ministry. As long as the persons involved see themselves as part of the leader's dream, sharing his heart, the dream will most likely continue to be realized and then expanded. When these people begin to feel that the dream itself has become more important in the mind of the leader than they are, the people who are helping him accomplish the dream, that dream has already begun to dissolve.

Ours is a day of shiftless people and shifting values. Our emphasis on a theology of success has produced people who are adept at dreaming greatly and often capable of seeing their dreams realized. Sadly, our lack of emphasis on personal integrity and Christlikeness has created a character vacuum in many of those same people. We are producing visionary heavyweights and character bantamweights.

Our secular society is all too willing to expose our bantamweight status. Consequently, for the good of the cause of Christ, we must pray for a return to personal holiness and integrity. We must ask God to grant us great character to support our great dreams. Our integrity must be of sufficient magnitude to undergird the unparalleled size of our accomplishments. If it isn't, the dream will implode.

Solid Living in Shifting Times

It is heartbreaking to watch a dream materialize and then disintegrate because it did not have adequate integrity to support it. People everywhere want to be identified with success. This is natural. The difference is that Christians are also desperate to be identified with a work that is pure, an identity that will give us a sense of service to Christ no matter what the actual job may entail. As the old hymn says, "In times like these, you need an anchor." And you need a very solid foundation.

Some years ago we built a new home. As the foundation was being laid, our builder advised us that we needed to "pour piers" into the foundation to steady it against erosion. Jesus admonished His followers to build their lives on the solid rock of unswerving loyalty and commitment to Him. The storms of life will batter a house, but it will stand strong *if* and only if it has the proper foundation.

Jesus said, "Whoever comes to Me, and hears My sayings and does them, I will show you whom he is like: He is like a man building a house, who dug deep and laid the foundation on the rock. And when the flood arose, the stream beat vehemently against that house, and could not shake it, for it was founded on the rock" (Luke 6:47-48).

Tragically, many dreamers proceed in building their super-structures without first laying the proper foundation. The only sufficient foundation is Jesus Christ. "For no other foundation can anyone lay than that which is laid, which is Jesus Christ" (1 Cor. 3:11). We must first trust Him as our Saviour, then allow Him to change us, remolding our character and redirecting our desires. As we lay the foundation of Christ's lordship over us, we should also be careful to pour the piers that will guarantee steadiness in shifting times. First, we should pour the pier of confidence in God's sovereign direction in our lives. There is nothing that brings such rest to the spirit as knowing that God is in ultimate control. It is unspeakably comforting to know that our lives, including all of our dreams, are in His hands — hands that were pierced for us.

Some years ago an elderly minister in an inner city area was walking home after his church's Sunday night service. He was suddenly accosted by a gang of young men bent on harming him. "Old man," they said, "we hate you. We hate your Jesus. We hate everything you believe. Now we're going to show you just how much."

The wise pastor was unafraid. Smiling, he replied, "No, fellows. You aren't in control of this situation. In fact, you can't do anything to me unless my Father gives your father permission." The gang quickly scattered.

Isn't it exciting to know that God holds us in His hands? And since we are held in His hands, the devil cannot bring anything against us unless it first passes through the hands of our heavenly Father. Let the pier of confidence in God's sovereign care be dug deep in your heart.

Then, pour the pier of an understanding of the grace of God. Nothing is transacted between God and people except on the basis of grace. In ourselves, we could never deserve the least of God's mercies. Yet He has chosen to be predisposed to love us and bless us as His children. His grace covers our sins and our failures. His grace is greater than our unrealized dreams. His mercy is extended even when dreams we have realized begin to collapse because of our own character flaws. The pier of God's grace reminds me that His mercy is constant and faithful, even when I am not.

Finally, pour the pier of a commitment to an ever-deepening relationship with the Lord. The apostle Paul had both seasons of triumph and seeming failure. Yet he said he learned to have peace of mind in either condition. "I have learned in whatever state I am, to be content" (Phil. 4:11). When the ultimate goal is Christ himself, not mere accomplishment, then our circumstances are much less important to us. Peter admonishes us to "grow in the grace and knowledge of our Lord and Saviour Jesus Christ" (2 Pet. 3:18). The ultimate goal, after all, is Christlikeness.

Have you experienced the agony of watching a realized dream disintegrate? Has your dream house been toppled? Your house-building days don't have to be over. As the Bible says, the "latter house" can be greater than the "former house," if you lay the right foundation and pour the right piers.

2

Life's Detours

*And we know that all things work together for
good to those who love God, to those who are the called
according to His purpose (Rom. 8:28).*

One night in 1978 I was pensively walking down
the historic lanes of Oxford. The still, crisp air,
cobblestone streets, and majestic colleges were a
beautiful setting for contemplation and prayer. As the old
hymn says, I sensed a "mystic, sweet communion" with
Oxford giants of earlier eras, people like John and Charles
Wesley and George Whitefield. More importantly, it was
one of those special times when the presence of Jesus
seemed particularly real and precious.

The whole scene lent itself to soul-searching, repentance, and adoration of the Lord. As I crossed the bridge
next to Magdalen College, I mused how God had used a
brilliant atheist-turned-Christian professor there. I was
thinking, of course, of C. S. Lewis. "Dear Lord," my heart
worshiped, "Your transforming power is so wonderful.
I'm amazed at how You can use one person's life. And his

influence seems even greater since his death."

It was a transforming moment, a prayer that seemed available to every Christian. "Lord," I prayed, "make my life like that."

Whether we're strolling the medieval streets of Oxford or darting through crowded traffic on our way to work, we all contemplate the impact our lives might make. We want to accomplish something significant, something noble, something that brings due honor to God. We want our lives to elicit some change or produce some effect that will tell future generations that we've been here.

We are born dreamers. God designed us innately to aspire to greater things. You never see children playing games of being poor, unnoticed, or insignificant. No, when children play "grown up," they project themselves into roles of importance. It is only as we grow older, after we have been sufficiently slapped into conformity by peers, family, religion, or society that we learn to be self-debasing. Those who dare to keep dreaming often do so at the risk of ridicule from friends and enemies alike.

Added to the threat of ridicule are the inevitable roadblocks that deter us from realizing our hopes. Instead of becoming discouraged and discarding our dreams, we should learn to look for the alternative routes around the roadblocks.

The apostle Paul learned to anticipate opposition whenever he aspired to significant strides in his walk with the Lord or in his work for Him. "So I find this law at work: When I want to do good, evil is right there with me" (Rom. 7:21;NIV).

Haven't you found that to be true? Whenever God plants a fresh seed of promise in your heart, there are immediate obstacles to its fulfillment. Jesus himself warned His followers that Satan specializes in "seed-snatching." He said, "The seed is the word of God. Those by the wayside are the ones who hear; then the devil comes and takes away the word out of their hearts..." (Luke 8:11-12).

If you are to see your dreams turned into reality, you must learn to guard the hopes God puts in your heart. And you must look for creative ways and alternative roads around the obstacles that barricade your progress. In John Bunyan's immortal classic, *Pilgrim's Progress*, the central character, Christian, had to determine to keep his eyes fixed on the Celestial City. The devil's cohorts conspired to distract him from his goal.

> *If you are to see your dreams turned into reality, you must learn to guard the hopes God puts in your heart. And you must look for creative ways and alternative roads around the obstacles that barricade your progress.*

Finally he stopped his ears to all of the clamorous distraction and ran toward the city, crying, "Life, life, eternal life!" In the same way, we must keep the eyes of our hearts fixed on the God-inspired goals He has placed in us. Like Bunyan's Christian, we must not be distracted by life's roadblocks or discouraged by its detours.

Let's look at some roadblocks to the fulfillment of dreams — life's detours on the path to realized hopes.

Unrealistic Expectations

A major barrier to the realization of some dreams is unrealistic expectations. This barricade, however, should not be viewed as an enemy but as a friend. Often valuable years of time are lost pursuing a vision that is not really our own. It was not born of God. At least it is not His dream for *us*, although it may well be for others. It is an imposed dream forced upon us by someone else's expectations concerning us.

I've seen this tragedy repeatedly in regards to vocational Christian ministry. Some well-meaning individual imposes his assessment of what another should do or be upon that individual. In my particular wing of the Church, we are especially vulnerable because we do indeed believe that God can give direction to one person through another. Sometimes we call this "directive prophecy."

Let me say first that I believe fully in present manifestations of the Holy Spirit such as prophecies, words of knowledge, and words of wisdom. But I must also say that in more than a quarter century of ministry, often I have seen a destructive pattern emerge. Most Christians deeply desire to know and accomplish God's will for their lives. If they're hazy as to exactly what His will is for them, they tend to be open to those who would give them guidance. Additionally, if their self-esteem is floundering, they are hoping for a word not only of direction but also of affirmation. Then when a well-intentioned spiritual person comes to them and says something like, "I can see you ministering to thousands," there's an obvious tendency to latch onto this encouraging chunk of hope.

Again, I want to emphasize that such a word can indeed be a word from heaven. But it might be just a word of human origin, a misread signal that is actually a distillation of one's own hopes for the person to whom he or she is ministering. Keen spiritual discernment is needed to know the difference. Let me give you an example.

Jack, a man in his early thirties, fresh out of Bible college with a wife and three children, worked the late-night shift in a suburban supermarket.

At school he had been challenged to "do something great for God." And his close buddy seemed to have a special understanding of what Jack's "something great" would be.

"Jack," his friend confided, "as I was praying for you this morning I seemed to see you in a little village with grass huts. The whole place was being transformed by your message about Jesus. Nobody had ever given them the gospel before you and your family got there. Man, you're not going to be sacking groceries forever. You're going to be carrying the Bread of Life. One day, probably real soon, you're going to be doing something *valuable* — something really *important !*"

A longing for noble accomplishment was sparked again in Jack's heart. And, of course, he correlated this directly to becoming a missionary.

About this time the night manager at the store recognized Jack's good work habits. He approached Jack about a possible promotion. He would be glad to recommend Jack for management training, he told him.

"Mr. Johnson," Jack replied, "I'm pleased that you would even consider me, but I can't be strapped here for six whole months of training. I'll probably be quitting pretty soon anyway. I'm getting ready to do something really *important.*"

Jack informed his wife not to pursue promotion at her job because they needed to be ready to go to the mission field, just as soon as the Lord opened the door. They would need to sell most of their furniture and not even think of buying a house. "We'd better not even sign a one-year lease," he cautioned his wife. So they kept their family in a substandard, crowded apartment — not because they were unable to live in a better place, but rather because they wanted to "stay mobile," as Jack put it.

In a couple of months Mr. Johnson approached Jack again. This time, it was not so amicable a meeting. "Jack, where are you? Your work is slipping. Customers are complaining. Employees are mad. You seem to be ten thousand miles away." Sadly, he was right.

"I've been thinking about what you told me awhile back," Mr. Johnson continued, "about probably wanting to quit. Well, friend, I'm going to give you a little shove in that direction."

That was four years ago. Jack has floundered from job to job. When he's home, he's depressed and distant. He battles for respect from his family. For the first time in their marriage, "divorce" slips into their strained conversations. Jack's wife is the major breadwinner. She talks frequently of her yearning to "get away for a little while." After she and the children leave for church, Jack curses one television preacher after another by remote control. "Why did You choose him, God, instead of me? I thought You didn't play favorites."

This tragic scenario didn't have to happen. Tough love would have confronted Jack with his true gifts, risking the backlash of his immediate anger in order to save him years of grief. Jack's skills and gifts were never in vocational ministry. He would have made an excellent supermarket manager. Had he ever gotten to the mission field, in all probability his effectiveness would have been minimal. But Jack tied purpose in life to being "in the ministry." He failed to see that nobility and purpose come from accomplishing *God's* plan for us, not someone else's imposed plan.

Jack's mistake was in assuming that his friend's picture of him as a missionary was on target. He did not stop to consider that it is possible to misread spiritual stimuli while in prayer or meditation, even in the integrity of our hearts. This is what happened to Jack's friend. He had a keen desire to see Jack "do something important for God." He wanted to see Jack happy and fulfilled. With the purest of motives, his own hopes for Jack were mistakenly viewed as a word from the Lord.

Years of agonizing frustration could have been avoided if Jack had known one simple thing: *It is extremely dangerous to try to force the fulfillment of a prophecy.* (Remember the trouble Abraham got into for that.) It is equally perilous to be too vocal and public about what God may whisper to us privately. Our response should be like Mary's response to the angel's announcement that she would bear the Messiah by a miraculous conception. "But Mary kept all these things and pondered them in her heart" (Luke 2:19).

We should take the precious hope and ponder it in

our hearts. If indeed the Holy Spirit birthed the idea, He will make it germinate and grow. The Holy Spirit can then bring that fully matured dream to pass.

Jack's detour (his store's management training) actually could have been the path to immense personal fulfillment for God's glory. But Jack couldn't see that. He was blinded by unrealistic expectations.

Uncooperative Circumstances

Probably the most common blockade to the fulfillment of our God-given hopes is uncooperative circumstances. As previously stated, the devil is already poised to throw broken obstacles on ambition's highway in an attempt to make our inflated hopes have a blowout. In this situation as well, Paul's inspired counsel comes to our aid.

This great apostle passionately pursued the highest of goals: Christlikeness. He looked forward to being conformed into the very image of Christ. Paul illustrated his quest as being not unlike the severe training of an athlete who "goes for the gold," with one important difference. For the athlete, the frenzied crowds would soon vanish. The cherished prize would be stashed away or, at best, hung as a memorial to past greatness. But not so with the prize Paul pursued.

Paul fully anticipated struggle, equal at least to the pain experienced by an athlete in training. But the very instruments of pain — those uncooperative circumstances — would bring growth, victory, and consequently approval both from the Lord and from the heavenly cloud of witnesses who cheered him on.

> Do you not know that those who run in a race all run, but one receives the prize? Run in such a way that you may obtain it. And everyone who competes for the prize is temperate in all things. Now they do it to obtain a perishable crown, but we for an imperishable crown. There-

fore I run thus: not with uncertainty. Thus I fight: not as one who beats the air. But I discipline my body and bring it into subjection, lest, when I have preached to others, I myself should become disqualified (1 Cor. 9:24-27).

As you pursue your heart's desires, uncooperative circumstances are to be expected. Jesus promised, "In this world you will have trouble." But He also promised, ". . . be of good cheer, I have overcome the world" (John 16:33). Mark it down: unfavorable winds will beat against you as you pursue your hopes.

To be truthful, these violent bellows and unfavorable gusts can greatly slow your progress. Such winds can slow you but they cannot ultimately stop you from reaching your goal. If the pursuit of your dreams is terminated, it won't be because of the adverse circumstances. It will be because you chose to stop when confronted with the uncooperative circumstances.

Unresolved Conflicts

Uncooperative circumstances cannot ultimately keep you from reaching your hopes, but unresolved conflicts can. Sometimes such conflicts are completely internal. The person never resolves his own inner suspicions about what he is pursuing. "Is it right?" he asks. "Is it right for me? Is it really God's will — for me — right now?" Because he cannot answer with ringing assurance, his pursuit is tenuous, spasmodic, and overly cautious.

The Bible admonishes us, "Let the peace of God rule in your hearts" (Col. 3:15). People too often pursue dreams they are uneasy about. The peace of God by no means rules in their hearts. If you are ever to see your hopes fulfilled, your heart must be at rest.

While some unresolved conflicts are purely internal, most unresolved conflicts involve someone else. Can you think of someone with whom you have an unresolved conflict? That unresolved conflict can potentially short-circuit everything God wants to do in and through your life. Paul said, "I myself always strive to have a conscience without offense toward God and men" (Acts 24:16). This should be your commitment as well. For without a clear conscience, cleansed by the blood of Jesus, you cannot fulfill God's purpose for your life. And if you are outside of God's will and, even more importantly, if you are outside of God's family, no amount of personal achievement can ever make up for the loss. "For what profit is it to a man if he gains the whole world, and loses his own soul?" (Matt. 16:26).

Our unresolved conflicts with other people cannot be resolved until we have first made our personal peace with God. Reconciliation between people must be predicated on reconciliation with God.

Have you experienced a personal reconciliation between yourself and God? Only on the sure basis of knowing that our sins against a holy God have been borne by Christ and thus forgiven, on that basis alone, can we aggressively pursue the reconstruction of broken relationships among ourselves.

If you don't know that all is well between you and God, it won't matter how many personal goals you achieve. Instead of tasting sweet, they will all turn to chaff in your mouth because what matters most in life is to know God.

Perhaps you have never opened your heart to Christ and received His wonderful forgiveness and cleansing. Or you may be unclear as to whether or not you have ever really committed your life to Him. Right now, wherever you are, you can turn from your past and surrender your future to Jesus Christ as Saviour and Lord.

If you will trust Him, Jesus Christ will completely transform your life. For the person who is following Jesus, the future is always bright, even if temporal circumstances are bleak.

One night I was talking to my neighbor. He had

recently come to Christ. The next morning he slipped me a note of encouragement that included these words:

> I felt like a failure, miserable and empty until . . . the Spirit entered my heart and said, "Go to Jesus. He is there. He blesses the weak. He came for sinners." The answer to disappointment is turning to Christ in prayer and letting him come and abide in us. I was sinking fast and was pulled up. If the blood of the Lamb was shed for the likes of me, a little disappointment or a big one can be dealt with.

That kind of transformation can happen to you as well. At this moment a new life can begin for you. You can experience complete forgiveness for your sins, serenity of mind and heart, and real purpose for living. On that foundation, you can rebuild your life.

Do you want this new life in Christ? Then make this the prayer of your heart:

> Lord Jesus, thank You for dying on the cross for me. Right now I repent of my sins and trust Your shed blood as the full payment for all my sins. I believe that You are the Son of God and that God has raised You from the dead. I now receive You as my personal Saviour and commit my life unreservedly to You as Lord. Thank You for hearing my prayer, forgiving my sins, and coming into my life as You promised. Amen.

If you prayed this prayer in sincerity and faith, welcome to the family of God. Like my neighbor, you will begin to experience a newness about everything in your life. Jesus Christ has promised to come into your life when, in repentance and faith, you invite Him to take up residence in you. The Bible says, "And this is the testimony: that God has given us eternal life, and this life is in His Son. He who has the Son has life; he who does not have the Son of God does not have life" (1 John 5:11-12). Now, through Christ, you have real life. God has forgiven you. On that basis you can now forgive others. Is God's Spirit nudging you right now about an unresolved conflict with someone? Why not make it right? Then you can get back on the road to real happiness and fulfillment.

Misplaced Desires

In this chapter you've already become acquainted with Jack. His story is like those of so many who misplace their aspirations. In the corporate world they refer to it as the Peter Principle: our tendency to promote effective workers to a higher level where they become ineffective.

One of our strongest needs is to be recognized and appreciated. This need is so powerful that we are often willing to fit into anyone else's plans for us, if there is the hope that we will be affirmed by them.

Take Donna, for instance. Donna's mother was very willful, opinionated, and aggressive. She carried some bruises from her own high school experience that were never fully healed, some personal dreams that never materialized. Subconsciously, she determined to vicariously fulfill those dreams through her daughter.

Donna's mother had always wanted to be a cheerleader and even football queen. She was neither. So she began to push Donna in that direction, first enrolling her in an expensive summer cheerleading clinic and then pushing her to try out as a cheerleader in the fall.

Donna was frightened by both experiences. She voiced a weak protest to her mother that was quickly silenced by the mother's threat of disapproval and a chilled relationship. And after all, Donna's mother reminded her, "I'm doing this because I love you."

Love should have seen, however, that Donna wasn't

interested in cheerleading. Donna's love was art. She could list the titles of each work by Dali or Van Gogh. But she didn't know last year's wins and losses or the names of this year's cheerleaders. Nor did she care to know. She viewed the cheerleaders as shallow and they viewed her as weird.

Yet for fear of losing the approval of her mother, she made an embarrassing attempt to enter the cheerleaders' world. She was soundly rejected. Her two weeks at cheerleading camp were a prison camp experience for her. She was fearful, hurt, and lonely. Then, because so much money had been spent on the camp, Donna felt forced to try out that fall. She stood petrified before the student body. Her flustered and somewhat uncoordinated attempts were met with heckling and some embarrassed silence from her classmates. It would take Donna years to recover emotionally.

In the epic film *Chariots of Fire*, the dean gave a stirring address to the incoming class of Caius College at Cambridge in 1920. He urged them to "find out where your chance for true greatness lies." That is very sound advice. If your chance for greatness is as an artist, don't pursue cheerleading. If your chance for greatness is as a mechanic, give yourself to that. If your chance for greatness is as a wife and mother, make that your first priority. Wherever God has given you ability or even budding interest, pursue that dream to greatness.

I went to college at a small Christian university in Arkansas. The founder of the school was a Methodist evangelist, John E. Brown. Early in this century he saw the validity of vocational training and was decades ahead of his time in educational techniques. Dr. Brown was fond of saying, "All work, done for the glory of God, is noble."

How I wish we could learn that! Then we would really believe that a garbage collector in the will of God is of far greater benefit to God and to society than a preacher who missed his true calling. Our self-worth and sense of personal dignity cannot rest on our involvement in a highly esteemed career. Rather, we must see the intrinsic worth of persons and understand, as Dr. Brown understood, that all work done for the glory of God, is noble.

This is so hard for many to realize — especially those who may be in vocational Christian work but shouldn't be. Peter warned church leaders to minister "not by compulsion but willingly" (1 Pet. 5:2). I fear that we have some in ministry today who were not called by God but by Grandmother. A love pat on the head and an affirming, "He's going to be a preacher when he grows up," is pretty powerful suggestion to a five-year-old.

In Martin Luther's day the church often taught that the only way to full assurance of salvation was to be a monk or a nun. Young Martin didn't care; he dreamed of being a lawyer. But when he was nearly struck by lightning and thrown from his horse, he instinctively vowed, "St. Anne, help me! I will become a priest!" Although history gives ample evidence that his entrance to the priesthood was sovereignly ordained, initially Luther saw his entrance into ministry as an obligation, a penance he had to undertake for his past frivolity.

While Protestants might deny that they have a system of penance, they, too, find ways to castigate themselves for past failures. I saw this repeatedly at seminary. We seem to imply to our young people, "Sure, you can honor the Lord in any work. But if you *really* want to serve Him, you'll go into the ministry." This has so infiltrated our subconscious that, in my neck of the woods, we even call it "surrendering to preach !" Do you see? In essence we're saying, "You poor sap. Just think about all you're going to have to give up. But, somebody's got to do it."

If a career in Christian ministry cannot be entered into with utter joy, it should be avoided. When it is seen as some kind of severe sentence, the prisoner will always dream of a jailbreak.

Your desires and goals should be in the direction of

what thrills your heart and imagination. Pursue that, to the glory of God.

The Enemy Within

Another massive roadblock to the fulfillment of dreams is that we discover that there is an internal war against noble desires. In William Golding's *Lord of the Flies*, a group of cultured British youngsters was shipwrecked on a deserted island. Stripped from the civilizing influences of the outside world, these prep school boys became savage in just a short time. Within weeks they had become barbarous and pagan. In a primitive hunt to track down the sinister force that was destroying them, they made a frightful discovery. "We have found the enemy," one wild-eyed boy exclaimed, "and it is us."

Paul spoke of this fervent inner struggle in the seventh chapter of Romans. Theologians continue to debate whether Paul is speaking generically or of his own literal struggle. And if it was his struggle, was he speaking of his pre-conversion dilemma or of a present struggle? We will leave it to the scholars to postulate answers. In any case, Paul poignantly portrays a battle with which much of the human race is all too familiar.

> For what I am doing, I do not understand. For what I will to do, that I do not practice; but what I hate, that I do. If, then, I do what I will not to do . . . it is no longer I who do it, but sin that dwells in me. For I know that in me (that is, in my flesh) nothing good dwells; for to will is present with me, but how to perform what is good I do not find. For . . . the evil I will not to do, that I practice. Now if I do what I will not to do, it is no longer I who do it, but sin that dwells in me. I find then a law, that evil is present with me, the one who wills to do good (Rom. 7:15-21).

The Apostle then goes on to present a solution through the dynamic, reconstructing power of the Holy Spirit. "The [principle] of the Spirit of life in Christ Jesus has made me free from the law of sin and death" (Rom. 8:2). That same Holy Spirit resides in you as a Christian to give you victory over the enemy within.

There are three manifestations of this internal intruder to the realization of our hopes. The first manifestation is *procrastination*. This is a kinder word for what earlier generations called sloth. Sloth is said to be one of the seven deadly sins. It is clearly satanic because it is a robber. Sloth robs us of our ambition, our time, and ultimately our very lives.

We must enter a go-for-broke struggle with procrastination. We dare not forget that our opportunities are fleeting. "For what is your life? It is even a vapor that appears for a little time and then vanishes away" (James 4:14).

We should adopt the posture of our Lord who squeezed a centuries-spanning infinity of ministry into three years. While He was never rushed or impetuous, He was always a perfect steward of time. "I must work the works of Him who sent Me while it is day; the night is coming when no one can work" (John 9:4).

With the Psalmist, our prayer should be, "So teach us to number our days, that we may gain a heart of wisdom" (Ps. 90:12). And, with Paul, we must vigilantly "redeem the time" (Col. 4:5).

A second clear evidence of the enemy within is *discouragement.* Someone has said, "The mark of a person's greatness is how much it takes to discourage him or her." Once a person begins to slip on the downward spiral of discouragement, he will soon find himself in the quagmire of self-pity. "Why did this happen to me?" will threaten to become his new watchword. Then it is only one short step to quitting altogether.

George Mueller was one of history's great people of

faith. He lived with the constant pressure of providing food, clothing, and care for the hundreds of orphans his hands of love had picked up off the impoverished streets of nineteenth-century England. Mueller knew that such a heavy responsibility would soon put him under if he ever acquiesced to discouragement. So Mueller learned to give the first few hours of each day to prayer, Bible reading, and meditation. He said, "My first assignment each day is to get my soul happy in the Lord." Make that the first priority of your day as well. Then you will not fall prey, at least not for long, to the venomous bite of discouragement.

It's always too soon to give up. Don't be discouraged in your work for the Lord. Remember, the war for this planet is fixed! Jesus shall reign. God has already decreed it. So it is impossible that any work in His name would be futile. The Bible admonishes us to be "steadfast, immovable, always abounding in the work of the Lord, knowing that your labor is not in vain in the Lord" (1 Cor. 15:58).

I remember one of my most discouraging days in India several years ago. I'd been gone for three weeks from my family and I was feeling the pangs of loneliness. One afternoon I was preaching to a convention of several hundred believers under a tent. It was hot, sultry, and windy. As I attempted to preach the wind would literally lift the tent off some of the poles. Of course, this was very noisy and distracting.

Then the photographer traveling with me stepped into the crowd. Sammy had red hair, a sight never seen by the Indians of this remote area. As he sat among them, many people lunged toward him to feel his hair. As Sammy focused the lens, the people around him began pointing and whispered in broken English, "Camera, camera!" And all of this was happening as I tried to preach!

Through the interpreter, I urged the people to refocus their attention on God's Word. I was preaching on the crowns and rewards the Lord will one day give for faithful service to him. I reminded them of the wonderful crown of rejoicing for those who win others to faith in Christ. (By that time, I certainly wasn't rejoicing.)

At that very moment, a young boy ran in from the back of the tent sporting a dead, four-foot snake he had just killed. He began to talk excitedly in Telegu and the people responded with shrieks and nervous laughter.

Again, I tried to restore order. The crowd again became somewhat subdued, although the distracting wind continued to spar with me for volume champion. Just as I was reaching the climax of the message, a cow walked right in front of the platform! I knew India was full of "sacred cows." This one was downright sacrilegious!

I just stopped, offered a short benediction, and made a quick exit to my hotel room. I was angry, embarrassed, and defeated. Never had there been such a barrage against my preaching. I sat numb in the sweltering heat, staring at the wall. I could not distinguish whether the little wet streams dripping down my face were tears or perspiration or both.

"Lord," I prayed, "I know You've said Your Word never returns void, but this sure seems like an exception. Why did it have to be me?" If ever I had felt like "hanging up my cleats" and quitting the ministry, it was that day.

The next morning I woke, still depressed, to the distant pagan chants of worshipers. We made preparations to leave and were walking toward the bus station. Suddenly I heard an excited voice behind me. "Dr. Shibley, Dr. Shibley!" the woman yelled as she ran in my direction. As the smiling woman hurried toward me an elderly woman followed at a slower pace.

"I just had to thank you," the Indian woman panted, half out of breath. "I heard what you said yesterday about a crown of rejoicing for winning people to Christ. I went home and said, 'Lord, I want that crown.' Well, I want you to meet my mother. I went to see her last night after your message. She is eighty years old and has worshiped false gods all of her life. I shared the message of Jesus with her and she immediately turned from her sins and idols and opened her heart to the Lord. Now she wants to renounce her old religion and receive Christian baptism."

Once again it was proven: God's Word *never* returns empty! It always accomplishes the purpose for which it is sent. Don't let discouragement take you under. You don't know the real impact you are making, even when it may look as though you are failing miserably. Fight the good fight of faith and don't turn back when you're confronted with the enemy within.

The third expression of this internal intruder to realized dreams is *doubt*. It is utterly impossible for dreams to be actualized without the inner confidence that they will be actualized. Of the many Christian virtues faith must rank very high on the list for the Bible says that "without faith it is impossible to please Him" (Heb. 11:6). With hope and love, it is an essential, abiding component of the believer's character.

I am not speaking here of a spurious confessionism that denies obvious difficulties. God may have made ostriches to stick their heads into the sand but He made people to be very much aware of what is going on around them. God honors great faith but He does not require us to deny reality.

There exists a pseudo-Christian cult built on the foundation of denying the obvious. I wonder if some true believers, who would never identify themselves with this group, aren't making the same mistake by denying the reality of pain and hardship in their lives. They fail to realize that the Bible does not say that having faith will eliminate difficulties and give prosperity in its place; it says God will help us through troubling times, whether or not He chooses to remove them. Few would deny that there have been sensational overstatements about faith by some well-known preachers. And the statements of these ministers have been stretched completely out of theological shape by some of their hearers.

At the same time, perhaps because of our extensive scientific achievements, we have come to lean on our technical prowess and believe only what we see. Thus we are the most skeptical or "faithless" age in history. In contrast to this "worldly" wisdom that demands visible data as proof, the great foundational plank of Christianity is none other than faith, invisible evidence that cannot be viewed through a telescope or studied under a microscope.

The result of these two extremes — the scientific impossibility of the supernatural, the religious denial of the natural — is a blending into an ineffectual sort of half-faith. The Christian cannot be "of the world" and thereby deny faith, but he may not wish to be labeled with some of the simplistic pronouncements of the prosperity message. So he settles, as some of the most ardent, Bible-believing Christians of this nation have, into a kind of "Christian rationalism" that wants to believe, but is hesitant to expect too much.

Don't let doubt or skepticism trip you up. You are not called upon to produce tangible evidence to "prove" your faith; nor must you deny the reality of your struggles. If God put a dream in your heart only faith can propel you toward its fulfillment. Accept His gift of faith. Keep your eyes on Him. Let your faith rise and, if need be, pray like the father who needed a miracle: "Lord, I believe; help my unbelief!" (Mark 9:24).

The Enemy Without

Not only do we have a vicious internal enemy; we have a strong external enemy. In fact, this enemy is ultimately behind every human heartache. This enemy is the devil and we cannot minimize his power. The Scriptures urge us, "Be sober, be vigilant; because your adversary the devil walks about like a roaring lion, seeking whom he may devour. Resist him, steadfast in the faith . . ." (1 Pet. 5:8-9).

A few of decades ago some very liberal, very foolish theologians were announcing that "God is dead." In contrast, by the sounds of some teaching today it would appear as though some thought the devil was dead.

Of course, biblically oriented Christians know better on both counts. God is the Ancient of Days but He is never old. He has always been alive and always will be. Satan, who is very much alive, has been on the job for quite some time as well — ever since his humiliating demotion from his high position as Lucifer, Star of the Morning, because of his treason and mutiny. He began working against God's purposes then, and will continue — at least until he is rendered ineffectual and cast into the bottomless pit.

The question of Satan's activities is one realm in which our imbalance is showing. On the one hand, some Christians lack discernment to see satanic designs behind their ineffectiveness. They attribute failure merely to circumstantial difficulties, personality conflicts, bad weather — anything, seemingly, except the devil. Jesus warned Peter, "Satan has asked for you, that he may sift you as wheat. But I have prayed for you, that your faith should not fail." (Luke 22:31-32). We dare not fail to see the hellish designs behind some, if not most, of our misfortunes.

Then, on the other hand, some Christians have swung to the opposite extreme. By their own admission they "see demons behind every bush." They fail to take into account simple factors like ignorance, misinformation, and willful sin as legitimate culprits. Flip Wilson's comedy character Geraldine excused every bad action by saying, "The devil made me do it." While this may sometimes be the case, more often than not the culprit is our own selfish will. We ourselves choose to live either after the flesh or after the Spirit. The Bible teaches that Christians are freed from the power of Satan by the blood of Jesus and the indwelling Holy Spirit. If a Christian is involved in sin, therefore, it is usually by choice and not by compulsion.

The story is told that President Teddy Roosevelt had

two pet dogs: a feisty little bulldog and a powerful Great Dane. Day after day, the bulldog would come into the Oval Office huffing, bloody, and snorting. He had picked yet another fight with the Great Dane and had been thoroughly humbled.

After several days of this repeated scrabbling, the president looked with amazement at his wounded bulldog. "What we have here is a lack of a healthy respect for the opposition," he chuckled.

We as Christians are to respect our enemy in the sense that we know he is deadly serious, fully set on destroying our lives. The Bible says that we are not to be ignorant of his devices. But while we are to take the devil seriously, we are certainly not to fear him. His ultimate demise is already assured. It is time for you to stand your ground, take your authority in Jesus Christ, and order the devil to step back: you're marching through!

You have an accuser, that is true. But you also have an Advocate. You have a diabolic enemy but you also have a divine Friend, who sticks closer than a brother. Satan, the enemy without, is bent on constantly blocking your progress. But keep walking. Don't ever retreat from him. In Jesus' name, he must retreat. The devil cannot defeat you unless you cower before him.

Sovereign Detours

There is one more roadblock we must explore. No doubt you've been down this road before. It's the sovereign detour. When you're there it seems like a cruel joke, but this heaven-sent barrier is God's act of love.

Because of the haste of our lives and the desire to reach our goals in the shortest time possible, we tend to view any impediment as a threat, an enemy to our progress. Most roadblocks can rightfully be viewed as such, but not this one. From time to time our hopes are re-routed by God, not by any negative design. Even though the detour may appear senseless to us, omniscient wisdom is behind it.

When I was nineteen years old the most beautiful girl I had ever seen just seemed to drop out of heaven into our little church in Tulsa. Physically she fit the bill I had already given to God: blonde hair, blue eyes, five feet four inches tall, beautiful smile. I thought God had *literally* answered my prayers. I got to know her and soon we were dating. We prayed together. We read the Bible together. For the first time in my life I thought I was in love.

Then, suddenly, it was over. Just as quickly as she had come into my life, she left. An air force pilot had stolen her heart and I was left heartbroken, confused, and angry. "What a cruel trick, Lord! I wasn't asking for her to just fall out of the sky one day. You did that. Why did You plant her here, first to lift my hopes, only to snatch them away?"

It may have been hard to deal with then, but I've been eternally grateful we didn't get married. Two years later I met Naomi. Now, my emotions toward the "blonde angel" were strong, but after meeting Naomi, I know the difference between mere physical attraction and genuine love. How thankful I am, in retrospect, for a sovereign roadblock to my own plans for happiness. Sovereign love always acts in our best interests.

You may be going through an experience that you feel is unspeakably cruel and unjust. But remember, it might be one of those situations in which, had you continued, you would have been annihilated by danger you couldn't even see. What may seem stern at the time is an arbitrary act of God's love.

A few years ago I met Dr. Robert Lindsey, then the noted leader of the Baptist House in Jerusalem. This humble man has an artificial limb. He lost his leg in a daring act of bravery and love.

As I recall the story, Dr. Lindsey saw a small Arab boy entering a minefield, oblivious to the danger around him. Instinctively, Dr. Lindsey darted toward the child, shoving him out of the danger zone just in time — for the boy but not for him.

The little boy didn't realize the magnitude of what had just happened to him. He felt hurt, intruded upon, forcefully shoved out of the way. He cried angrily because of the "mean man" who had thrown him out of the way into the dirt as he was happily playing. As the boy grew, however, his gratitude and admiration for Dr. Lindsey developed. In retrospect he realized that he owed his life to the gallant Christian pastor.

Have you felt forcibly shoved out of the way and into the dirt? Time and growth may reveal that your forced detour was a potent expression of God's strong, protective love for you. No experience for the Christian is indiscriminate or senseless. All of life, even detours, has a master design.

3

An Appointed Time

*To everything there is a season, a time for every
purpose under heaven (Eccles. 3:12).*

When our son Jonathan was in kindergarten his
teacher announced that the class would go in
two weeks to see a performance of *Snow White
and the Seven Dwarfs*. Each day for the next fortnight
Jonathan spoke excitedly about the upcoming event. His
whole life during those two weeks seemed to revolve
around the anticipated field trip.

The night before the class was to go to the play, we
received a call concerning an illness in the family that
needed our presence in another state. It would be necessary for us to leave immediately. Naomi and I told Jonathan
as tenderly as we knew how about the situation, explaining
how sorry we were that he would have to miss the play,
and that we would try to make it up to him, but that we had
to leave as a family and help our relatives. There was a long
moment of silence. Then Jonathan burst into one of the
most heart-rending cries I've ever heard from a child.

Have you ever felt that way? Have you ever edged right up to the fulfillment of a dream only to see your hope destroyed? It's never a joyful experience — it's usually a bitter one.

It's possible that in one sense it may be easier to have our expectations dashed completely, as Jonathan's were, than to have the dream postponed, only to come close a second or third time and have it postponed again and again. True, humans have a great deal of resilience and we can usually weather the disappointment several times. But if this goes on indefinitely, if we continue to get within grasp of our cherished hope, only to see it pushed out of our reach one more time, we become angry, or depressed, or shoulder a heartsick rejection.

For eleven years after my call to Christian ministry, I never lacked for opportunities to minister. Then, in 1977, I sensed a clear direction to resign my pastorate in Arkansas and go to seminary in Texas. Since I had many friends in Arkansas and knew virtually no one in Texas, I felt as though our family was being cast into a sort of wilderness.

This "wilderness experience" was accentuated when, after praying and hoping for preaching opportunities to open, it became painfully evident that I had to choose a means other than ministry to provide for the needs of my wife and son, with our second on the way, while I continued my classes.

I finally found employment as a shoe salesman for J.C. Penney. I determined to throw myself into my work and be the best salesman I could possibly be. Yet I felt like a fish out of water. For over a decade I had given my life to vocational ministry. Now it seemed that ministerial opportunities had come to an abrupt end. At the store I was courteous and maintained a veneer of cordiality to the customers. Yet every time I slipped a pair of shoes on another pair of feet, my heart was aching. I would go into the back room, looking for the correct shoe size and style, and realize that tears were starting down my face. "God," I whispered, "what am I doing here? I've heard Your call to do something else."

Multiplied millions of people go through the motions of making a living while agonizing in their hearts. "It's a living," they say, "but it's sure not a life." Long ago they had a dream that they may have dismissed as immature or foolish. Now they realize that dream was sent from God, but they are unsure how to go about fulfilling it or, like me in the shoe store, can't seem to make it happen.

Hope Deferred

The Bible says in Proverbs 13:12, "Hope deferred makes the heart sick." The world is filled with heart-sick people whose hopes have been jilted one too many times. While hope may indeed spring eternal in the human breast, it springs weaker after each deadline for fulfillment is postponed.

The Bible says we are saved by hope (Romans 8:24). The implication is that our lives have meaning and a reason for tomorrow based on the hopes inside of us. When hopes dim or disappear altogether, our vision for the future often dims as well.

We are an "instant" generation conditioned to quick solutions. Ours is a nation used to instant coffee, instant potatoes, and instant retrieval — within seconds we pull encyclopedias of information onto a computer screen. We see complex human dramas solved in an hour's time on television. We are geared to think that there should be a quick fulfillment of all our hopes.

Matthew Arnold spoke of how time diminishes hopes:

> *I feel her finger light*
> *Laid pausefully upon life's headlong train —*
> *The foot less prompt to meet the morning dew,*
> *The heart less bounding to emotion new,*
> *And hope, once crushed, less quick to spring again.*[1]

What an apt description of jaded desires! Just why are so many of our hopes deferred? There could be any number of reasons — and some of them may be sovereign — but three reasons seem to stand out.

First, as has already been stated, the problem could be the dream itself. We may be pursuing the wrong dream. Consequently our hopes are deferred simply because their fulfillment would cause confusion and disappointment both to ourselves and others.

A second possibility is that the timing isn't right. I frankly believe that we are entering an era where it will be crucial that believers know how to hear the voice of God in their spirits. Most of us, however, are much more skilled at hearing *what* God wants us to do than we are at hearing *when* and *how* He wants it done. For as surely as God has a will concerning what He wants done, He also has a strategy for its accomplishment.

We can mistake an impression concerning God's will as His green light to immediately pursue its fulfillment. Could this be why so many dreams He puts in us are stillborn? Many God-planted dreams are miscarried because of an untimely birth. The dream must be given time to grow and develop. Otherwise, even if it is birthed, it may be so premature that it must fight for survival when God intended it to be a natural, healthy delivery.

Not only is improper timing a possible reason for the postponement of our dream's fulfillment, improper strategy is also a possibility. Abraham's story is a case in point. How much better off Abraham would have been had he waited for God's strategy after he received God's promise. But a lot of time had elapsed since God had promised Abraham a son. He wasn't getting any younger, nor was Sarah. And besides, God might mistake Abraham's faith for passivity. Surely, such a circumstance demanded *action*, Abraham and Sarah thought.

So a brilliant strategy was conceived. Sarah would "deed" her maid, Hagar, to her husband for the purpose of childbearing. (There's nothing new under the sun. The idea of surrogate mothers is thousands of years old.)

It is interesting that Abraham was quick to accept this proposed arrangement. It might have passed through his mind, "Such a deal! I can help God out while becoming intimate with a beautiful young woman. And all of this with the approval of my wife!" It seemed like a win-win situation. How could he lose? He could retain his honor, assist the fulfillment of God's purpose, and satisfy his flesh all at once.

But something went wrong, drastically wrong. When the maid, Hagar, became pregnant by Abraham she began to despise Sarah, and Sarah responded by mistreating her. Hagar bore a son, Ishmael, and also received a promise that his descendants would be too numerous to count. (God later told Abraham that Ishmael would be so honored because he, too, was Abraham's son.)

More than a dozen years later Sarah gave birth to Isaac, the son promised by the Lord. Through Isaac the Jewish nation was established, and through Ishmael the Arab nations came into being. Scripture says that Ishmael's sons "lived in hostility toward all their brothers" (Gen. 25:18;NIV). In a sense, though God redeems all our blunders if we let Him, the world is still reaping the consequences of Abraham's action. Thank God, the final assessment of Abraham's life is that "he did not waver at the promise of God" (Rom. 4:20). Nevertheless, Abraham's "family feud" continues to the present.

When God plants a dream in your heart, watch out! You are very vulnerable. For quite often, on the wings of God's idea, will come *your* idea of how to get the ball rolling. This is an important time to check motives. Is the strategy heaven-sent, as well as the idea? Does the strategy appeal to your fleshly nature? Can others see the wisdom of God in the strategy as well as the idea?

The wrong strategy can set the fulfillment of your dream back years. Why? Because you may have to dismantle the apparatus of your old strategy before God sends you His.

Improper timing can set back a dream. So can improper strategy. But a third reason for the setback of many of our dreams is a lack of spiritual strength to birth the vision. Hezekiah lamented, "This day is a day of trouble and rebuke and blasphemy; for the children have come to birth, but there is no strength to bring them forth" (Isa. 37:3).

Ours is such a time. Many are pregnant with tremendous spiritual vision yet often there is not sufficient spiritual vitality to birth it. In a day when we show great interest in physical, mental, and emotional development, we dare not forget spiritual development. For the fact is that we are always either progressing or digressing spiritually. We are never just holding our own.

Before the births of our sons, Naomi and I attended prenatal classes to prepare and strengthen us for the upcoming births. Perhaps we need spiritual prenatal classes as well. Clearly some preparation must be made.

Part of that preparation is to live both in the reality of the present and in the hope of the future. Don't allow your hopes to dim because of postponement. The Bible says that God "calls those things which do not exist as though they did" (Rom. 4:17). So should you.

The Bible clearly states that Moses saw the coming Redeemer-Messiah and was thus strengthened for his task of leading God's people to deliverance. The Scripture says that Moses "endured as seeing Him who is invisible" (Heb. 11:27).

Abraham, as well, focused the eyes of his spirit and saw in the future what was unseen in the present. Abraham saw the Lord as Jehovah-Jireh — heaven's provision and atonement for sin. Jesus told His critics, "Your father Abraham rejoiced to see My day, and he saw it and was glad" (John 8:56). With the eyes of faith, Abraham saw a coming Saviour. He also saw a coming city. The Bible says that Abraham "was looking forward to the city with foundations, whose architect and builder is God" (Heb. 11:10;NIV).

Not only did Moses and Abraham see Him who is invisible, but notice how many times John says, "I saw," or, "I beheld," in the Revelation. And David, too, said, "I have set the Lord always before me" (Ps. 16:8).

Every believer should so envision the Lord. Paul said, "But we all, with unveiled face, beholding as in a mirror the glory of the Lord, are being transformed into the same image from glory to glory, just as by the Spirit of the Lord" (2 Cor. 3:18).

I fear there are many today whose faith is degenerating into a cold, rationalistic form of Christian philosophy. A great need in our day is for a hybrid believer who integrates solid evangelical doctrine with a deep, devotional spirituality.

Fidelity to the passages just mentioned mandates "beholding" the Lord as a biblical practice. As we seek Him, He will disclose himself and His ways to us. And as we seek Him, we will draw strength from His countenance. Thus we are enabled to birth the dreams He gives us.

If your hopes have been deferred, there's a reason. Check the hopes themselves. Then check the timing. How about the strategy? And do you have strength to birth the vision?

When my sister was about halfway through her second pregnancy, the doctor informed her that he had miscalculated. He readjusted the "due date" three weeks later than they had anticipated. I'm told by several women that such an announce-

> *Don't induce the birth of your hopes. Hope deferred is far better than hope destroyed because of inaccurate timing, improper strategy, or insufficient strength.*

ment can be an intense disappointment. Talk about hope deferred! Yet how much better for the health of both mother and child to allow the birth at the proper time rather than attempt to induce a birth when we *think* it ought to happen. Don't induce the birth of your hopes. Hope deferred is far better than hope destroyed because of inaccurate timing, improper strategy, or insufficient strength.

The Waiting Zone

Most of us have been guilty of praying, "Lord, give me patience — and give it to me *right now!*" I confess I'm often impatient. For instance, it's tough for me just to stand at a bus stop, unless I'm reading a magazine, reading a sign, reading people, doing *something* to keep from "wasting" my time.

I cannot verify this story, but I've heard it more than once. The story goes that Charles Wesley was cheerfully hoeing in his garden one day. Perhaps he was meditating on what would later become a grand hymn. A zealous young Methodist preacher questioned why Wesley would take time out for recreation when souls were fast slipping into eternity.

"Mr. Wesley," the young preacher asked, "if you knew Christ was returning in one hour what would you be doing?"

Wesley leaned on his hoe and thought for a moment. "I think . . . I think I would just keep hoeing my garden."

What is of ultimate importance is simply to be found doing the will of God at any particular moment. God's will for Wesley at that moment was to be tilling his garden. I know this is difficult for us activist Americans to understand. But part of the purpose of the waiting zone is for us to just learn to *be* in the will of God, before He releases us to *do* work for Him.

Time in the waiting zone is never wasted. It is an opportunity to concentrate on depth. The time will come later for breadth. In the waiting zone you simply learn to till your garden to the glory of God. You learn that there can be a touch of glory on the mundane occurrences of life when they are done in heaven's honor. It's a time when you learn to brush your teeth, read a book, take a walk, hear a symphony, and hug your kids — all to the glory of God. "Therefore, whether you eat or drink, or whatever you do, do all to the glory of God" (1 Cor. 10:31).

Some of your finest accomplishments will be in the waiting zone. For there the Lord is developing your character. There, because your dream has been postponed, your heart is sometimes crushed and those around you are the beneficiaries because whatever is in you, when you are crushed, will surely come out. And as the Lord builds His character in you, the life of Jesus will emit from you. "For we are to God the fragrance of Christ among those who are being saved and among those who are perishing. To the one we are the aroma of death leading to death, and to the other the aroma of life leading to life" (2 Cor. 2:15-16). When your dream is realized, your character will surely be tested. That is why character development must precede dream fulfillment.

Alexander Whyte was a godly Scottish pastor. Many young ministers in the waiting zone sought his wise and tender counsel. "Somewhere a congregation is awaiting you to be made by you," Whyte told them, "after you are made by God."

Are you in the waiting zone? Relax and let God work on your character. Your dream may have been deferred but it isn't dead. Deep in your heart your dream is being developed. And so are you. So go ahead and till your garden — with joy, not with tears. After your dream comes true you may seldom have time to garden!

One Thing Is Needed

If we are to see our dreams realized we must be sufficiently strengthened in the inner person where dreams develop. Often our spiritual weakness is directly linked to our shallow relationship with God. There is only one way to develop any relationship and that is to invest time in it. Prayer is the spawning ground of visions and dreams. And prayer produces the spiritual stamina necessary to come through the waiting zone.

Is there a dream in your heart that seemingly cannot become reality? Ask yourself: Was it conceived by God as I communed with Him? Then it must be brought forth the same way.

One of the exciting things God is doing today is calling the Church back to prayer. Do you realize that this privilege of communion with the Almighty, that we often take so lightly, is a privilege unique to those who know Christ? While the majority of the world's population is made up of ardent, sincere followers of some religion, only those who have been born of the Spirit can dare to hope that they can actually have an audience with the King of heaven. Jesus emphatically stated, "No one comes to the Father except through Me" (John 14:6).

Early one morning before daybreak, I stepped out onto the balcony of my hotel room in a distant country for a time with the Lord. I drank in His presence as I worshiped and adored Him. Suddenly, our communion was disrupted by the piercing chants of fervent voices throughout the city. Their disciplined, sincere attempts at reaching God are repeated systematically each day of their lives.

My heart wept for them. "Lord," I whispered, "these precious people desperately want to be heard by You. But never in their wildest imagination could they conceive that You would personally communicate back to them, much less really love them." With a renewed appreciation for what Christ's blood had accomplished for me, I revelled in the unique privilege of the twice-born — communion with Almighty God.

Are you taking advantage of your exalted privilege as a follower of Jesus Christ? The waiting zone is a good place to cultivate your prayer life. And your dream, once birthed, cannot be sustained without it.

Jesus reminded Martha that "one thing is needed," and that is to sit at His feet. David said, "One thing I have desired of the Lord, that will I seek: that I may dwell in the house of the Lord all the days of my life, to behold the beauty of the Lord, and to inquire in His temple" (Ps. 27:4). David wanted to stay in the house of the Lord because, under the Old Covenant, that was where God's presence resided. Paul said, "This one thing I do, forgetting those things which are behind and reaching forward to those things which are ahead, I press toward the goal for the prize of the upward call of God in Christ Jesus" (Phil. 3:13-14). Like Mary and David, Paul realized that the one thing that is needed is to fix our eyes on the Lord.

John Wesley said, "You can do more than pray after you have prayed, but you can do nothing but pray until you have prayed." In the waiting zone, you can learn the one thing that is needed. When your vision comes to pass, your activity will be vastly increased. You will fight a daily battle for time with Jesus. So God is giving you the opportunity to set your priorities now. In the future there will be many things that will be pressing and urgent. You may fight almost constant interruptions. But then, as now, only one thing will be absolutely necessary. Only through continued and deepened communion with the Lord will your dreams be able to expand and materialize.

Waiting on the Lord

It is often difficult yet always precious to wait on the Lord. When you're in the waiting zone, don't wait purposelessly. Wait on the Lord. God's Word promises, "But those who wait on the Lord shall renew their strength; they shall mount up with wings like eagles, they shall run and not be weary, they shall walk and not faint" (Isa. 40:31). When your dream is realized you will surely need endurance. The Olympic runner does not develop endurance during the big event of his life. He has already developed his strength and stamina in solitary pain years before his public chance of a lifetime.

To wait on the Lord carries the idea of waiting on Him as a servant waits on his master; to be poised to respond to his slightest wish. Perhaps a contemporary picture would be of a well-trained athlete, sitting on the bench waiting eagerly for the coach to call him into action. This devoted bench-warmer ponders a hundred times if it is worth it to endure such strenuous preparation. "Why go through all of this? Will I ever get into the game?" he wonders.

Then, during the game the coach suddenly calls this back-up and sends him in to relieve another player. His name blares out over the loudspeaker. The crowd instinctively looks for his number in their programs. Now he is thankful for every practice play he ever grunted through. He knows he's ready. And, as if by sovereign intent, he's in the right place at the right time and makes a key play.

Five minutes ago he was an unnoticed bench-warmer. Now he's a hero. That key maneuver, which he had practiced so many times only before the eyes of his coach, is now executed to perfection before the eyes of thousands.

Are you on some obscure practice field of life, waiting for your big chance? It will come. And probably when you least expect it. So stay faithful in executing the basics. Your lonely practices are a time of pruning, a chance to trim away all that is unnecessary. You are being cut back but you are not cut off. Stay faithful even when the world isn't watching. You'll be ready when it is.

Suddenly . . .

One day the prime minister of Great Britain, William Gladstone, gave an impassioned, brilliant response to a formal written speech in the House of Commons. The members of Parliament sat spellbound as they listened to the prime minister. One approached him afterward, saying, "Mr. Gladstone, I was deeply moved by your extemporaneous speech."

The prime minister replied, "That extemporaneous speech, as you call it, was twenty years in the making."

Like costly wine, that which is brewing and being distilled in you will one day be poured out, in the fullness of time. David was just a shepherd boy minding his father's business. One day on an errand for his father David was promoted to the status of a national hero. It came suddenly. Unexpectedly. Years later Asaph would reminisce on the goodness of God to the king. "He also chose David His servant, and took him from the sheepfolds; from following the ewes that had young He brought him, to shepherd Jacob His people, and Israel His inheritance" (Ps. 78:70-71).

Stephen served faithfully but without distinction as a servant-deacon in the church at Jerusalem. Suddenly, one gruesomely eventful day, his practice of faithfulness to His Lord held him in the hour of his greatest crisis. For twenty centuries now Stephen's name has been associated with greatness. His martyrdom has been the prototype of courage for thousands of Christian martyrs who followed. Today we honor him, not only as an example of how to live, but also as an example of how to die.

Philip also served behind the scenes in that band of Jerusalem deacons. But suddenly he too was thrust into greatness. One day he was wiping tables for widows. A few weeks later he was preaching Christ to thousands with attending miracles. Today he stands as the pristine New Testament model for the ministry of the evangelist.

A few years ago I was a miscast shoe salesman with an aching heart. Today I am grateful for the lessons He taught me as I waited for His appointed time to re-enter the ministry. "The Lord is good to all, and His tender mercies are over all His works" (Ps. 145:9).

Are you waiting in the wings? There's an appointed time for you. Your life and the circumstances of history will intersect at the perfect moment. Are you prepared for the Coach to look in your direction?

4

The Fine Art of Forgiveness

And be kind to one another, tenderhearted, forgiving one another, even as God in Christ forgave you (Eph. 4:32).

We are fast becoming a nation of angry people. There seems to be a bitterness that floats insidiously just under the surface of so many people's lives. We seem so quick to pick a fight or take up another's offense. The astonishing crime level indicates that many are looking for a way to "get back" at a society that hurt them.

Look at our fixation with the movie characters like Rambo and the Terminator. Why do so many identify so vehemently with them? Isn't it because, like Rambo, we feel that we've been given the short end of the stick and we enjoy vicariously avenging those who have wronged us? It is good that we still have a sense of justice. It is reprehensible, however, that we do not feel that we can appeal to God as our judge and, if need be, avenger. Thus we become our own avengers. And the cycle of hate continues.

Some years ago I was in Lebanon. Many people don't realize that the Lebanese are some of the most gracious people in the world. Their country just has the misfortune of being caught in the wrong place at the wrong time in history. Most of the initial fighting inside the country was because of outside aggression from many sources. But now many Lebanese themselves have been swallowed up in what seems to be an infinite cycle of retribution. "Your brother killed my uncle. So I must avenge his death and kill your son." This mindset is not just Middle East madness. It is the way many people have chosen to live in every part of the world.

If we do not deal with our own hurts and disappointments, we can literally become a threat to society. Unresolved bitterness is the first step, in my opinion, toward mental and emotional imbalance. The axiom is true: Hurt people hurt people. Our nation is filled with unforgiven people who are unwilling to forgive.

People are desperate today for pardon, affirmation, and a new beginning. Yet they are often chained to their pasts by unforgiveness. My father was a man of immense kindness. One of the first qualities he taught me was the fine art of forgiveness and affirmation. As a small boy I remember him teaching me this verse:

> *A good thing to remember*
> *And a better thing to do*
> *Is to work with the construction gang*
> *And not the wrecking crew.*

Which crew are you working for? Do you work to reconstruct the lives of those who hurt you? Or do you periodically bring out the old wrecking ball and give them another slam broadside?

The High Cost of Unforgiveness

Unforgiveness is extremely costly. In fact, one might

say it is a luxury item. Perhaps that is why some people seem to luxuriate in it, not stopping to realize that they will pay for it in long, expensive installments.

Jesus taught us to pray, "Forgive us our debts, as we forgive our debtors" (Matt. 6:12). Then He commented on this phrase, so as to leave no uncertainty about what He meant. "For if you forgive men their trespasses, your heavenly Father will also forgive you. But if you do not forgive men their trespasses, neither will your Father forgive your trespasses" (Matt. 6:14-15).

Unforgiveness is extremely costly. In fact, one might say it is a luxury item. Perhaps that is why some people seem to luxuriate in it, not stopping to realize that they will pay for it in long, expensive installments.

Do you think Jesus really meant that? Or was He just speaking metaphorically? If you were a betting person, how much would you be willing to bet that He was speaking literally? If we really believe Jesus was speaking straightforwardly (and there can be no doubt that He was), the cost of bitterness is simply too high.

A prominent evangelist in the South had built his ministry around vitriolic attacks against liberals (both theological and political), sexual deviants, and, sometimes, even charismatic Christians. Then a few years ago he underwent a life-altering experience with the Lord. He seemed to be drenched in the love of Jesus. He confided that he now had to build a new support base because his former supporters were made up substantially of angry Christians. When their spokesman ceased to vent his anger (and theirs), many of these same supporters then turned their anger on the evangelist. He says he has learned that it is far more difficult to raise money for Christian causes on a platform of love than it is to raise money on a platform of anger. How indicting.

This same evangelist related a very interesting story. He said that some time after his transformation he was approached by a warlock, the leader of an occultic group of Satan worshipers. The devil worshiper told him, "We've had to stop trying to put hexes and curses on you."

"But I preach the same gospel. I'm against the same devil," the evangelist responded. "Why should you stop trying to stop me?"

"Because since you started preaching this 'love your enemies' business, all of our hexes on you backfire and boomerang on us," the warlock retorted.

Evidently even wicked spirits took notice of the change in this preacher's attitude toward his enemies. Love *is* stronger than hate. It's the most powerful force in the world. No wonder Jesus said, "Love your enemies, bless those who curse you, do good to those who hate you, and pray for those who spitefully use you and persecute you" (Matt. 5:44).

Could it be that unforgiveness opens the gates for evil spirits to attack us? And could it be that real forgiveness, from the heart, spoils the intentions of the devil, freeing us and binding the powers of darkness? The answer, of course, is yes.

When the Hurt Won't Go Away

You may be reacting, "But you don't know how badly that person hurt me." It's true, I don't know, but I have seen a lot of hurt people. For instance, my schedule involves a lot of traveling and when I'm driving late at night, I'll sometimes take a break at a roadside cafe. Invariably, I see many divorcees working as late-night waitresses. It's the only shift they can work and be at home in the day to be with their young children. Many have left their children either with a friend or with their own parents while they work all night, after working at home all day, only to repeat the process again tomorrow.

I admit I tend to get angry with this generation of men

who so easily abdicate responsibilities as husbands and fathers. I've watched these women, many of them battling fatigue and depression, and I've thought, "This country has a lot of men who are real jerks." But then I catch myself. I must never reinforce any bitterness in myself or anyone else because that is never the road to healing and a new beginning. Bitterness is a bondage. It forces you to live mentally in the past and blinds you to the future.

Jesus gave a four-step escape out of the bondage of bitterness in the verse we just read. He showed us exactly how to respond to those who have hurt us, even when the hurt won't go away. The Lord said, "Love them, bless them, do good to them, pray for them." First, Jesus said we are to *love them*. It must be emphasized that the Lord is not requiring us to have some gushy feeling concerning them. Here love is a concrete, rational decision. It is not made because it will be reciprocated, necessarily. It may be that your love will not be returned in kind. Remember, angry people hung Perfect Love on a cross. Love, in this case, is a choice. It is offered not only because it frees the other person, but because it also frees you. When you choose to love those who hurt you, you release both them and you from the wages of their actions toward you.

God's love toward us was a rational choice. The Bible says that "God demonstrates His own love toward us, in that while we were still sinners, Christ died for us" (Rom. 5:8). God took the gamble of loving us *before* we ever responded to His love. He does not love us because we are good. He loves us because *He* is good. "Beloved, if God so loved us, we also ought to love one another" (1 John 4:11).

"But I *can't* love him," you might be saying. "I can't forgive him. I've already tried. I just don't have the capacity." How right you are. And what an excellent position you're in to receive divine ability. The Scriptures teach that we are laborers together with God. If we will simply give Him the right to love through us, then He will take it from there. The Bible says that the love of God is poured out in our hearts by the Holy Spirit (see Rom. 5:5). Won't you give the Holy Spirit the liberty to pour the love of God through you, beginning now, toward that one who hurt you?

Jesus then taught that we are to *bless them*. James warned Christians against verbal abuse (even when our target is *in absentia*) saying that the tongue is "full of deadly poison. With it we bless our God and Father, and with it we curse men, who have been made in the similitude of God. Out of the same mouth proceed blessing and cursing. My brethren, these things ought not to be so" (James 3:8-10).

You have the power to bless. When you bless those who curse you — literally speaking a word of God's favor and blessing to them — you render their curse against you ineffectual. I don't believe it misrepresents the interpretation to broaden it a bit. When you bless those who hurt you in the past, you can render the consequences of their actions toward you ineffectual as well.

Next, the Lord said to *do good to them*. This implies that there is some kind of contact with that person. If you are intentionally avoiding the one who hurt you, you may be entrenching the hurt. Of course, there are some circumstances where it may not be wise to enter back into someone's life; for instance, it is often best not to reappear frequently if one's former spouse has remarried.

In general, however, it is wise to look for ways to do good to those who have hurt you. A Christmas card, a phone call, a letter of forgiveness, flowers on their special days — these are seeds of reconciliation. Go ahead. Stop waiting for them to make the first move. Even if you're rebuffed when you reach out, God is recording your actions. You will never regret doing good.

Finally, Jesus taught us to *pray for them*. Perhaps the Lord put this last in the order because it would be hypocritical to pray for someone we had not truly forgiven. Often if we pray at all concerning those who have hurt us, we are not praying *for* them, we're praying *against* them. "Make him repent, Lord. Do whatever You need to do to show him the error of his ways." We're hoping, of course, that "whatever He needs to do" will be something drastic that will "teach him a lesson." Come on, now. Aren't you glad you're not God? And aren't you glad we're dealing with a God whose predisposition is mercy — toward all of us?

Sometimes the hurt is so deep that it may never go away entirely. There are emotional dynamics that may be beyond our control, no matter what steps we take. But the bitterness and unforgiveness *do not* have to stay. You will determine that. It will be your choice to forgive or not to forgive. Even when the hurt won't go away.

Absolving Those Who Hurt You

Every person alive has been wronged and thus wounded at some point in their lives. That means that we're all candidates for bitterness. Once we are wronged the ball is no longer in the court of the one who wronged us; the ball is in our court. How will we respond?

You see, nothing that happens to you can ultimately hurt you. Only your *reaction* can ultimately hurt you.

As has been stated, Jesus taught us to bless and not curse those who have hurt us. I have found in my own life that I must deal ruthlessly with anger before it takes root in my heart. Whenever I begin to think on the hurt, I choose rather to think on the Lord and His forgiveness of me. This is a conscientious choice that I alone can make.

What fills your mind is entirely up to you. You can, if you so choose, run thousands of "instant replays" on the hurts of your past. Or you can choose to fill your mind with the goodness of God. This was Paul's advice to the Philippians. "Finally, brethren, whatever things are true, whatever things are noble, whatever things are just, whatever things are pure, whatever things are lovely, whatever things are of good report, if there is any virtue and if there is anything praiseworthy — meditate on these things" (Phil. 4:8).

Jesus had plenty of reason to vent what would have been legitimate wrath as He was dying on the cross. And He had the option to do it. He could have dispatched vast garrisons of angels who were poised to come to His aid. But He *chose* not to avenge himself. Rather, He allowed His blood to continue to spill out of His body as an atonement for our sins. He chose to forgive. "Father," he cried, "forgive them, for they do not know what they do" (Luke 23:34).

You can choose now to absolve those who have hurt you. It's up to you. If you're willing to let go of your anger, and forgive from your heart, I want to help you. If you do not have the words to pray your own prayer, pray this suggested prayer. But in either case, pray out loud, sincerely, from your heart. You need to hear yourself forgiving the one who hurt you and speaking blessing on him or her.

Father, I come to You only on the merits of the Lord Jesus, who shed His blood that I might be forgiven. Right now I choose to forgive [the person's name] for all he/she has done that has hurt me. I ask You to forgive [the person's name] as well. I now absolve [the person's name] of all responsibility for my condition and I trust You and You alone to heal the wound in my heart. I thank You that, according to Your promise, since I have forgiven those who have transgressed against me, I will now be forgiven for my transgressions against You.

I now pronounce Your blessing on [the person's name]. I ask You to pour out heaven's choicest blessing on [the person's name]. In Jesus' name I pronounce blessing on [the person's name], on his/her spouse, [the spouse's name], and on their family.

In Jesus' name I now release them to a future

of joy and usefulness under the Lordship of Jesus Christ. And, in doing this, I am released as well. In Jesus' name. Amen.

Now, stop reading for a moment. Let the joy of the Lord flood your heart. Let His cleansing waves rush over you. It's a new day for you. You're learning the fine art of forgiveness.

Your Captivity Turned

If you continue to battle with unforgiveness, keep praying that prayer from your heart. Then you will notice things will begin to be different, because *you* will be different. Job had lost everything. His friends, instead of being true comforts, piled misery on top of misery by their pious accusations and verbal abuse. Naturally speaking, Job had every right to be angry.

But, instead, Job practiced the fine art of forgiveness. As soon as he forgave them, the miracle began. "And the Lord restored Job's losses when he prayed for his friends. Indeed, the Lord gave Job twice as much as he had before" (Job 42:10).

God is no respecter of persons. Job prayed for those who had hurt him. So have you. Job's captivity was turned. Yours will be too.

5

Recovering the Cutting Edge

Behold I will make you into a new threshing sledge with sharp teeth . . . (Isa. 41:15).

One of the most striking results of broken dreams is broken motivation. The will is simply uncooperative with aspirations of the future because of the pain of unrealized aspirations in the past. And, usually, the loftier the unfulfilled hope, the more reticent is the will to hope greatly again.

A clear evidence of this is my own generation. I went to college during what may have been America's most tumultuous years of national psychoanalysis: the late 1960s and early 1970s. Ours was the generation bent on changing what was perceived by many as a hypocritical social order. Many in my age bracket were ready to sit, march, riot, burn, and even die in order to raise the country's social sensitivities.

But where are these vocal zealots today? You will find a great many of them in pinstriped suits brokering stock in a system they once despised (and may still). These hippies-turned-yuppies have exchanged their plastic beads for gold necklaces and their faded blue jeans for designer denims. The junky van has given way to the sleek sports car.

You will notice that they often seem strangely mute in the face of a deadening indifference choking our consciences and general standards of decency and civilization. Having concluded from bitter disappointment that indeed you can't change the system, that you "can't fight City Hall," they practice a vicious capitalism in the office and a "leave-me-alone" hedonism during off-hours. For many, their highest "causes" now are enough cocaine to go around and ample benefits in their work packages.

What happened? Whether we agree with their former radicalism is not the issue. What is at issue is what demolished their determination and zeal for a better tomorrow. How did a whole generation whose slogan was "involvement" become today's uncommitted and uninvolved? The answer I continue to hear is profound in its simplicity. As a former ardent leftist told me, "Revolution is tiring." Evidently we are not wired to run on high octane for long stretches of time. While on occasion our fervor may be limitless in scope, it is usually limited in time.

Some time back I had lunch with a man who had engineered a national Christian conference in the early 1970s. He told me that many of the key players in that undertaking had become, in his words, "commitment casualties." He went on to explain that, in his estimation, it took about a decade for these ardent Christian soldiers ever to want to reenlist for any major cause or event. "They went full throttle for a couple of years. It just sapped their energies," he lamented.

Such is the description of untold numbers of visionary volunteers who, somewhere along the way, lost their thirst for battle. They just quit. Discouragement, failure, harassment, fatigue, or a wicked mix of these ingredients injected a deadly nonchalance into the once-alert and lively dreamer. It is true that dreamers are often naive. But naivete notwithstanding, only dreamers become achievers. Isn't it better to be a dreamer who wears rose-colored glasses than a skeptic who views all of life with a jaundiced eye?

The hopes of my generation have been largely unfulfilled. This has produced a weary acquiescence to the status quo. Frankly, I believe Isaiah was speaking prophetically of our day when he said, "Even the youths shall faint and be weary, and the young men shall utterly fall" (Isa. 40:30).

Swinging at Trees with Ax Handles

The Bible records the story of such a fervent young man who, at the height of passionate involvement, lost his effectiveness. Quite literally, he lost his "cutting edge."

This young man is described in 2 Kings 6 as a "son of the prophets." Either he was himself called to be a proclaimer of God's truth or he was the son of one such prophet. In either case he was under the tutelage of Elisha, God's powerful prophet. Elisha had himself apprenticed under the capable hand of Elijah. Now, because of his obvious prophetic anointing, young prophets were gravitating to Elisha. Apprenticeship was the educational norm of that day.

So rapid was the growth of Elisha's School of the Prophets that they soon outgrew existing dormitory space. At this juncture, one of the young men requested permission to lead an expedition of students to the Jordan River for the purpose of cutting down trees to build a larger resident hall, so to speak. Elisha gave his permission to this project and, at one student's request, even personally supervised the project.

Do you see it? Here's a group of godly young people with a clear vision. They are under proper authority. They taste the dream of an expanded ministry with its prospects for expanded influence. They are fervently at work in a noble and selfless cause. Their motives are honorable. Their hearts are pure. They are clearly enjoying the favor of the Lord.

Suddenly, the work of one young prophet becomes completely ineffective. His labor, though noble, is inept. With the best of motives and the clearest of visions, he loses his "cutting edge" in his work for God.

"But as one was cutting down a tree, the iron ax head fell into the water; and he cried out and said, 'Alas, master! For it was borrowed' " (2 Kings 6:5). The young prophet was unquestionably zealous in a good cause. With every swing he was thinking of the advance of God's purposes. He was happily at work in the service of the Lord. Though his heart was still in his work, his effectiveness was lost.

Today's unproductive servants could echo a similar sentiment: "I've become ineffective in my work; what's more, the effectiveness I enjoyed was loaned to me." They realize that any effectiveness they ever enjoyed was given to them by the Lord. Yet somewhere along the way, the sharpness of His power was dislodged.

It is a frightening thing to attempt ministry for the Lord in our strength alone. Nothing is more vital than the assurance of God's presence in our work for Him. When we sense that His presence or anointing for the task has lifted, our work is no more effective than if we attempted to cut down trees with ax handles.

Tragically, many individuals, churches, and even entire movements have lost the cutting edge. Though their love for the Lord and His cause may be as great as ever, there seem to be no results from what they are doing. When they take a swing at the obstacles in front of them, the obstacles don't budge. Nothing is shaken except the ardent workers themselves.

One day when I was eight years old, I was walking home from a baseball game. I had hit a home run so I was feeling good; my youthful adrenaline was whispering that I was invincible. I walked past the big oak tree in our neighborhood. I took my bat from my shoulder and mentally turned that tree into a baseball. The neighborhood became Yankee Stadium. I took a mighty swing and ... you can guess the result. My euphoria quickly faded as I stared at my now-splintered bat. Experience made me resolve to never take a swing at trees again.

So it is with many today. At one time or another they took a swing for the Lord, only to meet with disaster. The ensuing spiritual thud, produced by an unrelenting obstacle to their progress, discouraged them from ever taking another swing.

Have you ever felt that way? Do you feel that way now? You still love the Lord, but youthful ambition has given way to discouragement. Somewhere in your past you took a noble swing in His name and for His sake. Indeed, progress was being made, for a while. But one day, the tree — your obstacle — got the better of you. Your effort was fruitless; your cutting edge was lost.

At such a point it is futile merely to double your efforts or give your passion a pep talk. You must face the facts. Your effectiveness has gone. No amount of positive determination or positive thinking can change that. Yet many people and organizations keep the machinery running for months or even years because they don't want to assess the true situation. But if the cutting edge is to be recovered, you must make the same wise move as that young prophet. He stopped his activity long enough to accept the reality of his fruitless efforts. Then he went to his master with the problem and witnessed a miracle.

You, too, can tell your Master the truth of your fruitless service. He will not chide you or punish you. He knows the work you have put forth in His name. He also knows that in the heat of the day the devil often puts unbudging obstacles in the way to discourage you. As this young prophet did, come now to your Master and tell

Him the truth — that your service for Him, though well-intentioned, has become ineffective.

Ian Thomas tells how he voraciously served the Lord as a teenager. He attended every Christian event and was involved in endless good activities. But suddenly, at the age of nineteen, he felt completely drained, ready to give it all up. He complained bitterly to the Lord that he had done his best to spend and be spent for Him. Now he was spent indeed. His Bible reading was stale. His prayers were lifeless. His incentive had evaporated.

At this critical juncture young Thomas discovered the transforming reality of "Christ, who is our life" (see Col. 3:4). He began to see that he could exchange all of his weakness (and all of his strength) for the strength of Christ in him. He had found a priceless treasure. He had discovered, in his words, "the saving life of Christ."[1]

As you began your service for the Lord you had dreams of conquest and victory. Soon looming obstacles stood in the way. When you attacked them, you were shaken, not the obstacles. Your effectiveness had been temporarily dislodged. But it can be recovered.

Many ineffective servants, however, do not seem to make such a discovery. Instead, at this juncture, they call it quits. But the ax-swinging young prophet didn't give up. Nor should you. As you began your service for the Lord you had dreams of conquest and victory. Soon looming obstacles stood in the way. When you attacked them, *you* were shaken, not the obstacles. Your effectiveness had been temporarily dislodged. But it can be recovered.

Steps to Recovering the Cutting Edge

The story of the recovered ax head in 2 Kings 6 is more

than a historical narrative. Concerning these Old Testament accounts, the Bible says, "For whatever things were written before were written for our learning, that we through the patience and comfort of the Scriptures might have hope" (Rom. 15:4). This is not merely an accurate record of a miracle under the ministry of Elisha, although it is that. But this story also gives principles on how you too may recover effectiveness.

From this account of the lost ax head four principles emerge concerning how a cutting edge may be recovered after it has been lost. These principles are designed through the patience and comfort of the Scriptures to give you hope for a future that will be effective and razor-sharp.

Principle number one in recovering a lost cutting edge is that you must *go back to where you lost it.* "Where did it fall?" Elisha asked.

Where did you lose your effectiveness, your cutting edge? The question can be painful. Perhaps that is why we so often try to avoid it. We tend to say, "I don't want to take the agonizing trip back. I'll just get a new cutting edge." So we attend another seminar, buy another tape series or another book (even this one) hoping that some new insight will preclude our having to go back to the place where effectiveness was lost.

But this doesn't work. Not ultimately. You see, your "cutting edge" is unique to you. It is designed especially for you. A "new" cutting edge will not do. You must recover the original. And your original sharpness isn't really lost. It's exactly where you dropped it.

Have you ever dropped anything heavy into a running stream of water? If you have, you know that it is usually difficult to isolate exactly where it was dropped. But this was not the case with Elisha's student. In response to Elisha's question regarding where the ax head fell, "he showed him the place" (2 Kings 6:6).

There is a "place," some time or event in your past, when your cutting edge fell to the ground. In your own life, where did it fall?

Perhaps you may feel that you cannot isolate the exact place where your effectiveness was lost. "It was so long ago," you say. "So much water has gone under the bridge." But take another look. Look back into your past. The Holy Spirit will guide you to the exact time and circumstances.

How did you lose your cutting edge? Did you lose it by letting service for the Lord become more precious to you than the Lord himself? Many lose their effectiveness there. Ours is an activity-oriented society. It is easy to live under the tyranny of the urgent. The pressure, even from the pulpits, to "get up and do something for the Lord" has produced a choking "Martha complex" in many believers.

When Mary and Martha knew Jesus was coming to their house, they began to prepare for Him. Martha prepared the externals. Mary prepared her heart. When Martha saw Mary sitting enraptured at Jesus' feet, she became frustrated. "Why is she wasting valuable time while I'm busy trying to serve You?" Martha griped to the Lord. There's a direct parallel today in the lives of many well-meaning believers who are perhaps overcommitted to the work of the Lord and undercommitted to the Lord of the work. And have you noticed that today's Marthas are still upset with the Marys? Those who conscientiously develop their devotional lives risk being labeled as "passive" or "mystical" by their activist counterparts.

Is that where you lost your cutting edge? Did you lose it because, like Martha, you did not discern the difference between what is important and what is absolutely essential? No one questions that work for the Lord is important. But if we attempt service for Him without first being with Him, we will soon be swinging at trees with ax handles. God's Word promises, "Those who wait on the Lord shall renew their strength" (Isa. 40:31). Have you grown weary and ineffective in your work for the Lord because you charged into battle without even reporting for duty? Too often, instead of praying, "Here I am, Lord, send me," we must confess, "There I went, Lord. Rescue me."

If Jesus spoke your name once, you would surely stand at complete attention. But Jesus called Martha's name twice, lovingly commanding her full obedience to what He would say. "Martha, Martha, you are worried and troubled about many things. But one thing is needed, and Mary has chosen that good part, which will not be taken away from her" (Luke 10:41-42).

In a day when our entire society seems to be bowing to the false god of time and appointments, we need the counsel once again of the God who created time. He said, "One thing is needed," and that "one thing" is to be in His presence. If we do not sit at Jesus' feet to receive our marching orders from Him we may well become like the overly zealous runner who had no message to deliver although he arrived ahead of the others.

After years of dedicated, yet frustrating, missionary service in China, Hudson Taylor discovered that "one thing is needed." A vast ocean of needy humanity threatened to engulf him. The magnitude of need clawed for his attention each waking second. At first, Taylor attended to the tyranny of the urgent rather than the one thing that was needed before any other needs could be met.

Finally, after assessing his mixed bag of futile efforts and projects on shaky footings, Hudson Taylor, like Ian Thomas, discovered "the exchanged life."[2] He saw that he could exchange all of his inadequacies for the total sufficiency of Christ. He learned to first imbibe the Spirit of the Lord of the harvest before dashing off to work in His fields. Taylor's work became lasting indeed. Even today, one hundred years later, the Overseas Missionary Fellowship, which he founded, bears witness to one man who exchanged all that he could not be for all that Christ could be through him.

The insidious scheme of the devil is to divert our

attention, even just a few degrees, away from Jesus himself. Today we have an entire evangelical subculture, complete with our own magazines, seminars, colleges, recording and entertainment personalities, and publishing houses. One subtle way the enemy tries to divert us from Jesus is to enamor us with Christian things. Then, very subtly and with seeming innocence, our hearts are moved away from the Lord himself and begin to wrap themselves around things related to the Lord. Even service itself can then become idolatrous.

My father, a powerful preacher and Bible teacher, is now home in heaven. In the last year of his life, he had a recurring dream. He dreamed that he was in a crowded airport, running to catch a plane. As he hurried along the corridor, out of the corner of his eye he saw the Lord Jesus, sitting all alone.

Immediately, Dad would turn on his heels, forget about catching his plane, and sit down by the Lord. "Lord," my father would ask, "why isn't anyone paying attention to You? No one even seems to notice that You're here."

In the dream, the Lord answered Dad. "Everyone is so busy. In fact, Warren, you are so busy for Me that you're too busy for Me."

Do you know that can happen? It is possible to be so busy for the Lord that you're too busy for the Lord himself. Is that where you lost your cutting edge?

Or did you lose your effectiveness, perhaps, when you allowed bitterness to take root in your heart? When dreams don't come true it is easy to mentally stick the blame on someone else. "He could have given me the break I needed, but he didn't." "She ruined my reputation with her gossip." "That church never appreciated me." "He left me," or "She left me after I had given all I could give."

The writer of the book of Hebrews warns us to be alert "lest any root of bitterness springing up cause trouble, and by this many become defiled" (Heb. 12:15). Bitterness is cancerous to the spirit. It not only poisons the person in whom it is lodged; bitterness is a communicable disease. It can easily seep from one person to another. Notice that the Scripture says that bitterness can "spring up." Having been in ministry for more than twenty-five years, I have watched many aspiring leaders with fantastic potential become crippled by bitterness. When their vision did not materialize in the way or at the time they had hoped, disappointment was often allowed to fester into anger. Then anger grew internal roots which became long-standing bitterness.

In my opinion, more people are sidetracked at this point than at any other. Seemingly, one can more easily recover from the "major" sins than one can recover from bitterness. This is because bitterness takes root. Rooted deep inside, it waits insidiously below the surface. Then, when provoked, it springs up. That is why it is usually futile to admonish people to "stop being angry." Often surface anger is deeply rooted in internal bitterness. The cure for surface anger is not to stop being angry. The cure is to pull bitterness out by the roots.

This can only be accomplished by a deep work of the Holy Spirit — but the cutting edge can never be recovered until bitterness is ruthlessly pulled out by the roots. God seldom, if ever, greatly uses bitter people. You must go back to where you lost the cutting edge, identify the disappointment, then admit and forsake the bitterness that has ensued.

The Holy Spirit may impress you to ask forgiveness from those who have hurt you. God is in the reconciling business. And when we align ourselves with Him, we will be in the reconciling business too. So disregard that lump in your throat. Go ahead and make that phone call. Write that letter of apology. Set up an appointment with that estranged friend and ask his forgiveness for your unforgiveness.

Then, whatever the response, you will know that you have done what you can do toward restoration. Your heart will be free. You will have a sense of being clean. Then put the matter in God's hands. You will be on the road to recovered effectiveness.

Whether your effectiveness fell at the place of bitterness, mismanaged priorities, or at some other place of failure, to recover the cutting edge you must first go back to where you lost it. Though the trip may be costly, it is absolutely necessary. You must identify the source of your ineffectiveness.

The second principle in recovering a lost cutting edge is that you must *apply the cross of Christ to the place of failure and ineffectiveness*. The Bible says that Elisha "cut off a stick, and threw it in there" (2 Kings 6:6). The Hebrew word translated "stick" can refer to a large piece of wood. I believe this piece of wood is a type of the cross of Christ. Notice that Elisha applied the wood to the place of failure and ineffectiveness.

This is not the only instance in the Bible where something like this occurred. Exodus 15 tells us that Moses brought the Hebrew children to the waters of Marah. The people were desperate for water, but they couldn't drink the waters of Marah because they were too bitter.

For many, the cup of life's disappointments is too bitter to drink. The Bible records that "the Lord showed [Moses] a tree. When he cast it into the waters, the waters were made sweet" (Exod. 15:25). No matter how bitter the waters of your past may be, when you cast in the tree, that is, when you apply the cross of Jesus to the bitter experiences of your past, your bitter waters will become sweet.

Jesus not only transforms how we view our present; He also transforms how we view our past. When the blood of Jesus is applied to the broken pieces of our lives, even the deeper colors and stains can be seen as part of a beautiful redemptive mosaic. Each piece has been carefully inlaid by the Master Artist.

You may view past misfortunes as purposeless chaos. Take a closer look. Then stand back and look at the big picture. Those isolated ruptures of chaos have tremendous meaning as part of the whole master plan.

If you arrived late at a performance of Tchaikovsky's *1812 Overture*, you might only hear cymbals clashing and cannons blasting. You might be tempted to think, "This is nonsensical noise." But if you heard the composition from start to finish, you would realize that there was masterful logic behind what seemed to be unnecessary and discordant.

Are there some bars in the score of your life's composition that appear crude and worthless? Trust the Master Composer. When your life's symphony is completed, you will see that there was consummate skill and divine purpose even behind the inclusion of the cannon blasts.

The work of Jesus Christ in any human life is always redemptive. Of course, we usually think of Jesus' blood primarily as the agent of cleansing for our forgiveness and salvation — and this is wonderfully true. The Scriptures also teach that the blood of Christ continues to activate our relationship to God and to one another. "But if we walk in the light as He is in the light, we have fellowship with one another, and the blood of Jesus Christ His Son cleanses us from all sin" (1 John 1:7). The word *cleanses* could literally be translated "keeps on cleansing." The blood of Jesus Christ keeps on cleansing us from all sin. The Greek word for cleansing is the basis for our word *catharsis*. The blood of Christ has a cathartic or purgative effect in the believer's life. His blood continues to purge us from the bitter hurts and failures of the past.

Your effectiveness can be recovered. Go back to where you lost it and apply the precious blood of Jesus to your failure. He is waiting to cleanse you and give you a new start. His blood will actuate the needed catharsis to purge you from past failures and release you to new potential.

Third, you must *expect the miracle of a resurrected cutting edge.* After Elisha found the place the ax head had fallen, he "cut off a stick, and threw it in there; and he made the iron float" (2 Kings 6:6). It is naturally impossible for iron to float. All of the natural forces of earth mitigate against it. You may feel that it is equally impossible for your effectiveness ever to resurface. Indeed, all of the forces of life may seem to mitigate against that as well. But don't forget what Jesus said: "The things which are impossible with men are possible with God" (Luke 18:27).

God ordained natural law but He remains Lord over it. Therefore, at His decree, iron can swim. Every circumstance of your life may scream that your effectiveness is gone forever. But God can circumvent circumstances. He is the Lord over circumstances. At His command, your effectiveness can and will resurface.

I read recently of a Hanoverian countess who lived about a hundred years ago. She was a notorious atheist and was particularly offended by the doctrine of the resurrection of the dead.

The countess died when she was about thirty years of age. Before her death she gave orders that her grave should be covered with a slab of granite. Around the grave should be placed square blocks of stone. The corners should then be fastened to each other and to the granite slab by heavy iron clamps. (It's funny, isn't it, how many of those who say they don't believe in resurrection and judgment so aggressively fear it.)

This inscription was then placed on the covering:

THIS BURIAL PLACE,
PURCHASED TO ALL ETERNITY,
MUST NEVER BE OPENED.

Everything that was humanly possible was done to keep the grave sealed. However, not long after, a little birch tree seed sprouted and the root tunneled its way between the side stone and the upper slab. There it began to grow. Slowly but steadily it forced its way until the iron clamps were torn off the hinges and the granite lid was raised. Today the lid is propped open on the trunk of the large and flourishing birch tree.

It may be that everything has been done to ensure that your lost effectiveness stays buried. All of life may seem to conspire against your cutting edge ever resurfacing. But the power of God can rip the hinges off the opposition. There will be a resurrection.

Both in principle and in fact, for the believer, always after crucifixion comes resurrection. There is no biblical reference to crucifixion that does not then imply resurrection. After the cross, then the empty tomb. After the blood has been applied, then expect the miracle of resurrection. When we acknowledge that we are crucified with Christ, then we are raised to new life with Him. In the same way, when we allow His blood to purge our past failures, we can legitimately expect the miracle of resurrected effectiveness.

Finally, you must *reach out the hand of faith and take the cutting edge*. No doubt the young prophet stood in amazement as he saw gravity defied and his ax head reappear. He was probably speechless. Elisha shook him back to reality. The miracle was not for the purpose of amazement but for the purpose of renewed effectiveness. In so many words, Elisha told him, "Don't just stand there and gawk at the miracle. Reach out! Pick it up for yourself." Then the Bible records, "He reached out his hand and took it" (2 Kings 6:7).

One of the Hebrew words for *faith* means "to say amen." You have taken the steps to recovered effectiveness. God has commanded your cutting edge to resurface. Now, let your faith say, "Amen! I receive my recovered cutting edge now. Thank You, Lord!"

Wherever you are right now you can reach out in faith and receive the miracle of recovered effectiveness. It's yours. But you have to pick it up for yourself. It is my prayer that wherever you are right now you will pause and transact important business with the Lord. Take the steps now to recover your effectiveness.

Is It Too Late?

Perhaps you have been ineffective for a long time. You may wonder if your dreams, long since buried, can ever be recovered. Some remote sin of the past may not only mar your past but plague your present. Can you ever be fully effective again?

No doubt Moses asked that question a thousand times through his tears. Here was a man who in "righteous indignation" killed a man in cold blood, then ran from the scene of the crime. "God, how could You ever use me now?" Moses cried. "I'm a murderer. What can You do with a murderer?"

But today, he is not remembered as "Moses the murderer" but as "Moses the Lawgiver." As an octogenarian, when most men are preparing to die, Moses was launched into the most exciting era of his life. Moses' period of relative ineffectiveness lasted forty years. But then he recovered the cutting edge.

"It's too late" must have frequently raced through the mind of David. At the height of his authority and anointing he committed adultery. His anguished plea for restored fellowship with God is recorded in Psalm 51. Can you hear David as he agonizes, "Oh, Lord, how did this ever happen?"

I've heard it said that David undoubtedly gave way to an evil progression of lust that finally culminated in adultery. I'm not sure I believe that. I'm more prone to think that he just fell in one weak moment. After all, we are talking about a man after God's own heart.

There are many believers today who also grieve over moral failure. And they wonder, as King David did, how it ever happened. Their sin haunts them just as David's sin haunted him.

But today we do not remember "David the adulterer." We honor him as "David, the man after God's own heart." He allowed God to cleanse him thoroughly and give him a new start. "Purge me with hyssop, and I shall be clean," he prayed. "Wash me, and I shall be whiter than snow" (Ps. 51:7). There was a new beginning for David, and there can be a new beginning for you.

Perhaps you have let a past rejection crush you. Such could have been the case when a beautiful young Christian girl named Emily broke her engagement to a young evangelist. His name? Billy Graham. "One of two things can happen in a time like that," Graham said. "You can resist and become bitter, or you can let God break you. And I determined to let God have His way."[3] Billy Graham rose above the rejection and later met Ruth, God's wonderful choice for him all along. You, too, can rise above the rejection of your past.

Or you may have been wounded by tragedy. Perhaps a loved one has died and you can't seem to shake the grief. Elisabeth Elliot lost her husband, Jim, to the savage spears and hatchets of uncivilized Auca tribesmen.[4] Jim died in an effort to get the gospel to them. Elisabeth overcame the heartache and even allowed God to give her a deep love for her husband's murderers. She courageously took her young daughter and lived among the Aucas. Today, because of her witness, there are hundreds of Auca believers, and the Aucas themselves are evangelizing surrounding tribes. Elisabeth Elliot overcame tragedy. So can you.

It is not too late to recover the cutting edge. Your acquiescence to an ineffectual life is premature. "For I said in my haste, 'I am cut off from before Your eyes'; Nevertheless You heard the voice of my supplications when I cried out to You" (Ps. 31:22). It wasn't too late for the Psalmist and it's not too late for you.

You can recover the cutting edge today. Right now. Go back to where you lost it. Apply the cross of Christ. Expect the miracle of resurrected effectiveness. Then, by faith, reach out and take it.

6

The Vision Refocused

*Therefore I run thus: not with uncertainty. Thus
I fight: not as one who beats the air (1 Cor. 9:26).*

My first pastorate was in Possum Hollow, Arkansas. I'll never forget the wonderful people there. I'd drive south from Siloam Springs past Dutch Mills on the seldom-traveled two-lane highway. Then I'd take the dirt road past Mrs. Terrill's chicken houses for a little over a mile until I got to the small, white frame church.

Our Christian education department consisted of two Sunday school classes: children and adult. Randy would accompany me on the tinny-sounding upright piano as I led us out of our Stamps-Baxter songbooks. After I preached to my congregation of twenty-five or thirty, we'd pray fervently for needed rain or for Mrs. Whelan who was going into the hospital for tests. Then we'd take hands and sing "Blest Be the Tie." We would linger in the balmy Arkansas sun on the church grounds next to the cemetery with its monuments to slain Confederate soldiers. In every direction, all that could be seen were simple farmhouses, chicken houses, grazing cattle, and the dirt road.

Years before I got there, the little church had prayed for an opportunity to do something for missions. One farmer suggested that "there might be some preacher boy up at John Brown's college who'd want to come down here and learn to preach. He could practice on us." Since that morning in the early 1950s, ministerial students from John Brown University had gotten their first taste of the pastorate at the sympathetic hands of the folks from Possum Hollow. Not only did they get to preach, they earned a salary as well. By the time I arrived in 1970 I was taking back to campus a much-appreciated fifteen dollars a week.

What was even more appreciated was Sunday dinner! These salt-of-the-earth farmers took turns inviting the preacher home for fresh catfish or (of course) fried chicken, complete with turnips, potatoes, and strawberries fresh from the garden with whipped cream fresh from Elsie, the family cow.

Nourished by the food, the simple goodness of the people, and the sincere worship, I'd return to the church for my Sunday afternoon routine: a leisurely prayer-walk through the cemetery, Billy Graham's *Hour of Decision* on my car radio at 3:00, and a nap on a wooden pew at 3:30.

A church with no real problems where the people love you and each other. Who could ask for more?

I could. Lots more.

Balancing Our Needs

Every person has two distinct needs: Security and significance. Of the two, the one that is more pressing at any given time is the one to which we gravitate. If our more pressing need is for relationships we will move toward people and places that help fulfill our security need. To some extent all of us identify with Thoreau. We all want a personal Walden, a sort of fictional Mayberry where life is uncluttered and the town's worst social ill is Otis' seemingly harmless drunkenness.

But if we are fairly secure, or if we are highly motivated, we move more in the direction of significance; we want our lives to make a difference. So we gravitate toward people and places where we feel we can make an impact. Goodbye Mayberry, hello Dallas!

The real trick is to hold these dual desires in tandem. Often we sacrifice one for the other. In the 1960s many people said farewell to the "rat race," opting for a lifestyle of simplicity and, it was hoped, security. Today there seems to be a reverse trend. We seem enamored of the lifestyles of the rich and famous. We want — we need — to be noticed. The hippies' answer to depersonalization was to retreat and "get back to oneself." Our answer seems to be to make a big enough splash that people will notice us, thus affirming our personhood.

Now that you are recovering your cutting edge, it is time to refocus your vision. In the recovery of your lost (or submerged) hopes, you can find both security and significance. But remember, no matter how lofty the dream, there is no lasting security that forfeits relationships. Nor is there any lasting significance that treads on people.

Some time ago I watched a remake of the old TV show "This Is Your Life." The lives of two famous comedians were spotlighted. As relatives, bosses, and casts from their pasts came to share the remembrances, I realized again that what is most important in life is not lasting limelight but lasting friendships. So if your dreams put you in the fast lane, take the back road every now and then to Mayberry. The folks in Mayberry will help you keep the city's glimmer in perspective.

Back to the Original Vision

I pray that hope is being rekindled in you as you read. As poet laureate Carl Sandburg noted, "Nothing happens unless first a dream." Is the Holy Spirit stoking the smoldering ashes of dreams you had lost? Let Him continue to kindle the flame and bring you back to the original vision.

I've observed that a person's greatest anointing is usually on his original call. Though our influence and interests may broaden, we are tragically mistaken if we assume that God's blessings and anointing automatically transfer to all of our endeavors. For instance, Moses was anointed to inspire and lead, but he needed lessons in group management from his father-in-law, Jethro.

In the same way, you will usually find that your greatest anointing is for that area where you are naturally gifted and initially called. It is, of course, quite possible for the Spirit's anointing on us to expand or even shift areas. Witness, for example, when a successful evangelist becomes a successful pastor. (By the way, many successful evangelists fail as pastors.) The successful evangelist-turned-pastor will inevitably be an *evangelistic* pastor. His evangelistic anointing follows him into his new endeavor.

> *You will usually find that your greatest anointing is for that area where you are naturally gifted and initially called. What great thing were you once called to do? What's to keep you from still accomplishing it, even after all these years of stalls and disappointments? Is the calling still there? Yes, it is. "For the gifts and the calling of God are irrevocable" (Rom. 11:29).*

Do you remember your original dream? Perhaps you wanted to be a lawyer, an interior designer, or a master mechanic. Who first planted that dream in your heart? In all probability it was God. He only desires what will affirm and bless His children. As surely as God is pouring out His Spirit around the world, He is causing old men to dream dreams and young men to see visions (see Joel 2:28). What great thing were you once called to do? What's to keep you from still accomplishing it, even after all these years of stalls and disappointments? Is the calling still there? Yes, it is. "For the gifts and the calling of God are irrevocable" (Rom. 11:29).

You may feel exasperated regarding your desire. Perhaps you are frustrated not only with yourself but also with God. Habakkuk poured out a bitter complaint before God. He told the Lord frankly that the vision God had promised had not come to pass. The prophet said, "O Lord, how long shall I cry, and You will not hear? even cry out to You, 'Violence!' and You will not save?" (Hab. 1:2). The embittered prophet then proceeded to chronicle his complaints to God for showing him a vision of a nation at peace with her neighbors and with her God when the fulfillment of the vision was elusive. After questioning out loud why pagan nations prospered at Judah's expense, the prophet said, "I will stand my watch . . . to see what He will say to me, and what I will answer when I am corrected" (Hab. 2:1).

The angry preacher had finally been brutally honest with God. Now he braced himself for the heavenly rebuke he thought was inevitable. But God did not rebuke His spokesman. God is not taken aback by our honesty before Him. In fact, it forms the basis of communication with Him. As long as we retain our reverence for Him, God literally welcomes our questions — even angry ones.

Instead of rebuking Habakkuk for his questions, the Lord reaffirmed the vision. Just as the prophet was ready to scrap the vision as a delusion, the Lord buttressed his sagging hopes. "Write the vision," He answered the prophet, "and make it plain on tablets, that he may run who reads it. For the vision is yet for an appointed time; but at the end it will speak, and it will not lie. Though it tarries, wait for it; because it will surely come" (Hab. 2:2-3). In other words, when the time is ripe, nothing will be able to stop it!

Has your once-flaming vision dimmed to a faint and distant longing? Should you then discard the vision altogether? No! Go back to the original vision. And adopt the formula for fulfillment that God gave His prophet.

First, God said, *write the vision*. Perhaps you have been too nebulous in articulating the vision. Write it down. Describe exactly what you see in your heart. The act of putting it on paper somehow makes the vision more concrete to you. It is imperative that you write the vision.

Second, *clarify the vision*. God commanded His spokesman, "Write the vision and make it plain." We should be able to distinctly describe our purpose and our vision for accomplishment. Decades after his Damascus road conversion and call to ministry, Paul was able to recall clearly God's unique mandate to him before a government inquisition. Paul chronicled his conversion to Christ and the words of the Lord to him:

> I am Jesus, whom you are persecuting. But rise and stand on your feet; for I have appeared to you for this purpose, to make you a minister and a witness both of the things which you have seen and of the things which I will yet reveal to you. I will deliver you from the Jewish people, as well as from the Gentiles, to whom I now send you, to open their eyes in order to turn them from darkness to light, and from the power of Satan to God, that they may receive forgiveness of sins and an inheritance among those who are sanctified by faith in Me. Therefore, King Agrippa, I was not disobedient to the heavenly vision (Acts 26:15-19).

Paul was perfectly clear concerning God's purpose for his life. You, too, should have a clarified vision.

Third, God told Habakkuk to *read the vision*. After the vision was clearly defined and written, it was to be read repeatedly. This would indelibly imprint the vision in both the heart and mind. We are transformed (literally, metamorphosed) by the renewing of our minds. And this mental renewal takes place by massive doses of the Word of God. This is not only a reference to Scripture memorization and meditation; we are to meditate on God's special word *to us*, His unique vision for us that He speaks to our hearts.

Once you have clearly defined and written the original vision, put copies of it on your mirror, in your purse or wallet, in your Bible, or on the dashboard of your car — anywhere and everywhere you can to keep the vision freshly before you. You see, we naturally move toward whatever is directly in front of us. That is why it is vital to read — and keep reading — the vision.

Finally, God told the prophet to *run with the vision*. In other words, he was told to move purposefully toward its accomplishment. When a God-breathed, clearly defined vision is fixed in the mind of the aspirant, he will naturally run toward its fulfillment.

Every time you read the vision, it is like stoking the embers in a heart on fire for the will of God to be done. So take the prescription for fatigued hopes. Go back to the original vision. Write it. Clarify it. Read it. Then read it again. And again — until the flame soars brightly in your heart. You will notice that your heart is beating more quickly. Spiritual adrenaline is pumping. You're running, once again, toward the vision.

The Whole Purpose of Man

My father used to tell me, "It is more important what God does in you than what He does through you. Because the quality of what He does through you will be determined by what He does in you." As you begin again to run toward the refocused vision, remember to retreat to your personal Mayberry for inner renewal and continued character development. As Jesus, the Master of time management (and everything else), told His followers, "Come aside by yourselves to a deserted place and rest a while" (Mark 6:31). During such times of spiritual repose, we regain our inner equilibrium and reaffirm once again those things that are of ultimate importance.

Some time back I was graciously hosted by the world's largest church, the Yoido Full Gospel Church of Seoul, Korea. This church of half-a-million plus members is the largest single congregation in the history of the Christian faith.

In preparation to preach at the Friday all-night prayer meeting (which was jammed with more than ten thousand people) I was taken to the church's Prayer Mountain, close to the infamous 38th Parallel. I then was invited to spend a couple of hours in the personal prayer grotto of the pastor, Dr. David Yonggi Cho.

As I crawled into the little tomblike cubbyhole in the mountainside, I realized that I had indeed "come aside to a deserted place." But I found that this "deserted place" wasn't deserted at all. It was filled with the presence of the Lord. As I communed with the Lord there, I refocused on lasting things. "Lord, what's of ultimate importance? What *really* matters in life?" He impressed three simple things upon my heart. Above all else, what ultimately matters is that we know God, that we walk with God, and that we accomplish the will of God.

I challenge you, first, to know, genuinely know, God. Then walk with Him. If you know Him and walk with Him, you will surely accomplish His unique design for your life. How wonderful to be able to say with Paul, "I have finished my course; I have accomplished God's will for me."

The Westminster Shorter Catechism says it this way: "The whole purpose of man is to glorify God and to enjoy Him forever."

Through an amazing set of circumstances I became close friends with the late Paul E. Billheimer, author of

Destined for the Throne and several other contemporary Christian classics. Shortly before Paul's death, the Holy Spirit impressed me that he would soon be going to heaven. I flew out to his apartment in Los Angeles to see this godly, aged saint one more time. He was bedridden, so weak he could manage only a few words at a time. Naturally I clung to every syllable from the lips of this dying prophet.

After prayer together I stood to bid him farewell. Painfully he lifted his hand and motioned for me to come nearer. He harnessed the strength to give me his final words of counsel. I strained to listen deeply to the parting words of one of this century's giants. I knew what he said would be a distillation of sixty-five fruitful years of service for his King. His voice almost gone, he had to yell to whisper. With tears in his eyes (and mine), he said, "David, all . . . that matters . . . is Jesus. *All* . . . that matters . . . is *Jesus.*"

7

When It Can't Be Fixed

Nevertheless My lovingkindness I will not utterly take from him, nor allow My faithfulness to fail (Ps. 89:33).

It was the phone call that would change my life. I was fifteen. On the other end of the line my mother was weeping. "David," she said, "you'd better sit down." I knew instinctively what was coming. "Your dad just died." I felt keenly sensitized and completely numb at the same time. I stumbled for half coherent words. "You're sure? There's no mistake?"

I walked in a daze around my cousin's neighborhood. I had stayed with him that week while my father fought for his life in the hospital. As I walked, oblivious to the surroundings, I began the nauseous process of reprogramming my life without my father.

I asked to be taken to the church my father had pastored for the last ten years. I walked to the front and lay face down in front of my dad's pulpit. I knew that in a couple of days my father's body would be lying there as hundreds would gather to pay tribute to him. Throughout the afternoon I writhed in agonizing prayer before the Lord. I blurted repeatedly, "Why? Why us? Why me?"

Two weeks earlier I had made a no-strings-attached commitment of my future to the full lordship of Christ at a Christian camp. I knew Dad was dying. I also knew God could heal him. I had reason to hope He would. One of my last conversations with him was to tell him of my all-out commitment at the old-fashioned camp altar.

That picture flashed before me as I lay prostrate at the church. "Lord," I reiterated, "I wasn't kidding. I gave You complete authority over my life at that camp. I meant it then. I mean it now, even though I don't understand."

Over the next few months the finality of his passing sank in with deadening impact. Since Dad was a minister, it wasn't too unusual for him to be gone a week or even two at a time. But this time he left and didn't come back. Nor would he ever return.

My faith and hopes for his healing had been canceled. I juggled the delicate theological process of discarding my faith for his healing without discarding my faith in God's power to heal. I sorted through the tangled paradoxes of sovereign choice that allowed my father to die, and sovereign benevolence that was supposedly always in effect. Of course, at fifteen, I didn't use these words. But I grappled with these issues nonetheless.

I was faced with an irretrievable dream. It couldn't be fixed. Dad wasn't coming home. He *was* home — in heaven. My dreams of growing up in the security of my father's care would not come true. There would be no more father-son banquets. I would always want to rush past Father's Day from then on. Every morning I would wake to a stark new fact: My dad is dead.

I knew my "defense mechanisms" were building walls of callousness to protect me from ever being hurt that deeply by loss again. I seemed powerless to halt their construction, yet as quickly as they were put into place, I was able to dismantle them. Somehow I knew that such walls would not protect me but rather imprison me.

Then there was the new role. I could no longer afford the luxury of just being a teenager. I had to grow up. I was the closest thing my two younger sisters would have to a father figure. *Responsibility* took on a much greater meaning. A popular song of the time certainly applied to me: "The times, they are a-changin'."

Yet, in spite of all this, in the midst of my inner chaos there was an anchored calm. The faith of my father was also mine. I too had trusted Christ. And I trusted what He said: "He who believes in Me, though he may die, he shall live" (John 11:25). I determined to be true to myself and to God — about my future, my anger, my questions, my newly sprouting hopes, my fear ever to love deeply again. "Behold, You desire truth in the inward parts, and in the hidden part You will make me to know wisdom" (Ps. 51:6). The truth was, Dad had died. The truth was, I hurt. The truth was, I didn't know where to go from there.

Have you been at that place? What do you do when life takes a sudden, disastrous turn and the events that made it happen cannot be recalled?

The Humpty Dumpty Syndrome

A lot of people could identify with Humpty Dumpty. From their elevated positions, they had a great fall. Like Humpty their brokenness seems beyond repair. And all of the care and concern in the world seemingly can't put the broken pieces back together. When personal dreams are trampled, the possessors of those dreams feel trampled as well. Under the pounding hooves of life's tragedies, we feel like echoing with William Yeats, "Tread softly because you tread on my dreams."[1]

When we absorb the shock of irreversible tragedies, no amount of human consolation is ever quite enough. Though we may be very appreciative of the support of others, the ache goes deeper than the ability of human help to heal. At such times of irrevocable loss, the only effective salve is the Balm of Gilead, the Lord Jesus. And the only precursor of lasting peace is the blessed Comforter, the Holy Spirit.

> *After we have been broken by the hard realities of life, like Humpty, "all the king's horses and all the king's men" may not be able to put us together again. But the King can.*

We somehow know that, though friends sympathize, only our Friend who sticks closer than a brother can fully empathize. As Jesus looks down at our distress, He is not a dispassionate observer. I love the old Authorized Version rendering of Hebrews 4:15: "For we have not an high priest which cannot be touched with the feeling of our infirmities; but was in all points tempted like as we are, yet without sin."

After we have been broken by the hard realities of life, like Humpty, "all the king's horses and all the king's men" may not be able to put us together again. But the King can.

Just the Facts

In the old television series "Dragnet," Sergeant Friday was adept at keeping witnesses centered on only those items that were germane to the case. Friday was fond of saying, "Just the facts, ma'am, just the facts."

What are the facts — just the facts — when the villain of loss has stripped away all contingencies? What is left of faith when it is distilled to its essence? What can one know for certain when he or she is deprived of wealth, position, health, and family — all in one day? Job experienced all of these tragedies. His pain was augmented by heartless "comforters" and an unsupportive, bitter companion. Certainly, if we have experienced tragedy, we can learn from someone like him.

Most Bible scholars believe that Job lived in remote antiquity. He probably lived in a culture where Sabeanism (the worship of stars and planets) was predominant. Accosted by such paganism, and plagued with the most depressing of circumstances, what did Job know without question?

Job pronounced his "just-the-facts" statement of faith in the midst of unspeakable compounded tragedies. He declared, "For I know that my Redeemer lives, and He shall stand at last on the earth; and after my skin is destroyed, this I know, that in my flesh I shall see God" (Job 19:25-26). Let's dissect this faith at its essence.

First, Job knew he had a Redeemer. He knew that heaven would provide One who would redeem him from present trouble and future judgment.

Second, Job knew that his Redeemer was alive. Job's Redeemer was not a concept but a living Being, sympathetic and fully capable of lifting those who are cast down.

Third, Job knew that his living Redeemer would ultimately triumph. He would "stand at last on the earth." When the final tally is taken, Job knew that his Redeemer would conquer.

Fourth, Job knew that death is not the final chapter. Though death would terminate the functions of his mortal body, he would still see and experience the presence of God.

Fifth, Job knew that he would experience a physical resurrection. "In my flesh," he said, "I shall see God." The eternal destiny of his body was not corruption but glorification.

Finally, Job knew that he would see God. No trial is too difficult if we really know that, when all is said and done, we will see God and He will see us. As the old hymn says, we will be "safe in the arms of Jesus."

Perhaps you, like Job, live in an environment that is hostile to your faith in a living Redeemer. Your friends may be less than supportive. There may be angry denunciations of your stand within your own family. You may have been pelted all at once with hell's heaviest arsenals.

At such a time, when faith is boiled down to what you know without question, take heart. You still have a triumphant, living Redeemer. *That* assurance can never be taken away.

When the Scales Don't Balance

"But why me?" you may be asking. "Why have I been singled out for heartache and loss?" Of course, you haven't been singled out. The loss of health, the loss of financial security, the death of a loved one, the termination of relationships that were supposed to last forever — sadly those are frequent human agonies. Even as you read this book tragedies are pounding millions of unsuspecting families.

We are often told these days to "take charge of your life." And to a certain extent you can and should. To a large degree you can determine how much you will weigh, how wisely you will invest your money, how you will spend your free time. But you cannot determine who around you will die. Or when. You cannot mandate the attitudes or words of others regarding you. You cannot simply "choose" not to acquire some terminal illness. Such contingencies are beyond your control.

What you can control is your response to such assaults. And your response will be determined largely by what you know for certain about God, your relationship with Him, and your future with Him.

Elizabeth Skoglund recounts the importance of remembering the eternal dimension when we suffer:

> In my work as a counselor I see many who feel hurt from unjust criticism, for the idleness and, indeed, savagery of words can be felt as a very deep form of suffering. But perhaps those who feel the most criticism at times are those who are in positions of power, particularly in Christian work. A leader in the Christian world

is troubled by a disturbed child. Instead of being upheld he is often criticized by fellow Christians. Illness is regarded as lack of faith in some circles. Men earnestly helping with the emotional problems of their congregation find themselves suddenly accused of a sexual affair. For such the words, "Nothing matters but that which is eternal" is at times the only effective antidote.[2]

We must remember the words of Scripture, "For our light affliction, which is but for a moment, is working for us a far more exceeding and eternal weight of glory, while we do not look at the things which are seen, but at the things which are not seen. For the things which are seen are temporary, but the things which are not seen are eternal" (2 Cor. 4:17-18).

The piercings of your heart can be transformed into the skillful scalpel of the Master Surgeon and the tempered pruning hook of the Divine Husbandman. Annie Johnson Flint expressed this truth so well:

> *It is the branch that bears the fruit,*
> *That feels the knife*
> *To prune it for a larger growth,*
> *A fuller life.*
>
> *Though every budding twig be lopped,*
> *And every grace*
> *Of swaying tendril, springing leaf,*
> *Be lost a space,*
>
> *O thou whose life of joy seems 'reft,*
> *Of beauty shorn;*
> *Whose aspirations lie in dust,*
> *All bruised and torn,*
>
> *Rejoice, tho' each desire, each dream,*
> *Each hope of thine*
> *Shall fall and fade; it is the hand*
> *Of love Divine*

That holds the knife, that cuts and breaks
With tenderest touch,
That thou, whose life has borne some fruit
May'st now bear much.[3]

Don't judge your tragedies as meaningless. Learn to view life's heartaches from an eternal trajectory. "Therefore judge nothing [no heartache] before the time, until the Lord comes, who will both bring to light the hidden things of darkness [not only our shortcomings but also our sorrows] and reveal the counsels of the hearts. Then each one's praise will come from God" (1 Cor. 4:5).

The Bible's Reality Therapy

When our hopes evaporate, the key to maintaining our sanity, both emotionally and spiritually, is by coming to grips with the reality and permanence of our loss. As Elizabeth Skoglund said, "In real life only children believe that pain always goes away; and even they learn quickly that such is not the case. Only the insane achieve in actuality the eradication of all pain; and they do it by denying reality, not finding it."

Habakkuk had to come to grips with the fact that some of his dreams would not come true and that some of his losses were irretrievable. With rational objectivity coupled with spiritual optimism he assessed his losses and mapped out his emotional response. "Though the fig tree does not bud and there are no grapes on the vines, though the olive crop fails and the fields produce no food, though there are no sheep in the pen and no cattle in the stalls, yet I will rejoice in the Lord, I will be joyful in God my Savior. The Sovereign Lord is my strength; he makes my feet like the feet of a deer, he enables me to go on the heights" (Hab. 3:17-19;NIV).

This is a good description of what I call the Bible's reality therapy. In this passage the prophet chooses how he will approach the loss of the past, the attending pain of the present, and the potential of the future.

First, the prophet accepted the past. He came to grips with the permanence of his loss: "The fig tree will not bud." That for which he had hoped was not going to materialize. He knew that and accepted it.

Then, he embraced the present. In spite of his loss Habakkuk made a willful choice concerning his present response. He refused to live in present defeat because of past calamities. All of his surrounding circumstances pointed to a very bad year indeed: crop failures, cattle sterility, and other disasters. But, like Job, he could not be robbed of his communion with God. Setting his face like flint against the winds of adversity, the prophet chose to rejoice in the Lord and be joyful in God his Saviour.

Embrace the present goodness of God. Steel your will and choose to rejoice, not in your loss, but in your Sovereign Lord. If you determine to stay riveted to willful worship, you may be only hours away from a new beginning.

Finally, Habakkuk determined to run toward the future. He determined to focus on the joy ahead of him, not the pain behind him. He knew that, in the not-too-distant future, the Lord would enable him to "go to the heights."

Many people choose to retreat from the future, choosing rather to nurse old wounds. Others simply resign themselves to the future. But not Habakkuk. He anticipated the future with joy. Not only would he laugh and smile again. He would even skip again, just as he did as a child. "He makes my feet like the feet of a deer."

Take this biblical prescription for new hope. Accept the past. Embrace the present. Run toward the future. A new day is dawning for you.

After my father died I chose to swallow this scriptural medicine. And although I continued for months to cry myself to sleep, God was weaving new dreams into my heart as I slept. One morning as I awoke I was very conscious that the birds were singing God's praises. And so was I. My heart was brimming with new hope and joy. The sorrow was still there, but joy had triumphed.

The misfortunes of your life may be legion, but if your faith stays intact, there's a future for you. There is omniscient wisdom even in the midst of permanent loss. As Alexander Maclaren said, "The only real calamity in life is to lose one's faith in God."

8

Your Alabaster Box

Pour out your heart before Him:God is a refuge for us (Ps. 62:8).

In the seventh chapter of Luke there is a beautiful story of one woman's lavish offering of devotion and sacrifice. "And behold, a woman in the city who was a sinner, when she knew that Jesus sat at the table in the Pharisee's house, brought an alabaster flask of fragrant oil, and stood at His feet behind Him weeping; and she began to wash His feet with her tears, and wiped them with the hair of her head; and she kissed His feet and anointed them with the fragrant oil" (Luke 7:37-38).

Many Bible commentators feel that the alabaster box was given to her while she was still a young girl by her parents as a dowry. It was probably ceremonially presented to her in a shared, joyful anticipation of the husband who would someday come, and the prospect of grandchildren.

But life had taken a tragic, ugly turn for this girl. The husband never came. The children never came. Instead she was trapped in a dehumanizing web of hurt and sin.

Then one day she met a Man unlike any other, a Man who could actually remit sin and give new life. She began to follow Him. She laid before Him all of the sordid realities of her scarred life. Her sins were forgiven; her life was transformed.

Now that she had abandoned her lucrative profession, she probably had little she could offer financially to the Lord. Yet her love for Him demanded that she continue to probe her heart. Was there anything — anything else she possessed — that she could lay before the Lord?

Then she remembered. Back at her little dwelling, in an obscure corner gathering dust, lay her alabaster box. Each time she saw it her heart ached with remorse and regret, but she kept it nonetheless. It was her only link to a life that might have been. The alabaster box symbolized for her those cherished dreams that never came true. This transformed woman realized that, although she had laid before Jesus all the things in her life that she wished had not happened, she had not yet given Him the secret longings of her heart, the things she had *wanted* to happen that did not.

She hurried home and retrieved the alabaster box. Perhaps she paused and wept one more time as she held in her hands this token of her unrealized hopes. The Bible then records her reverent oblation as she poured out her precious offering before the Lord. As she spilled out her last link with past hopes, she was being changed and freed, her critics notwithstanding. For this lavish offering she received accusations from the self-righteous, but accolades from the righteous One himself.

There are many people who have given their lives to Christ who have not yet given Him their unrealized hopes. They have laid before Him the life that actually is, but they have yet to pour out before Him the life that might have been.

The Life That Might Have Been

Have you given to Jesus your unfulfilled dreams, your life that might have been? I contend that you cannot be fully free until you do. Although you have given the Lord your life, and consequently have received forgiveness and a new life, total freedom will come only when you break your alabaster box at His feet.

Somewhere in the recesses of your heart you keep an alabaster box. Take your secret box of dreams — your deposit, if you will, on your inheritance that never came in. Pour out your hurts before Jesus. Empty every ounce of the precious contents on the feet that were pierced for you. Then linger, as the woman did, to worship Him.

Somewhere in the recesses of your heart you keep an alabaster box. Perhaps you avoid seeing it except on rare occasions. Like an old family picture album, it conjures up both precious memories and regrets; sweet thoughts you want to remember and painful longings you're trying to forget.

Take your secret box of dreams — your deposit, if you will, on your inheritance that never came in. Grieve again, if you want to, over those dreams that never came true, but do so in the presence of Jesus. Pour out your hurts before Him. Then open the box. Empty every ounce of the precious contents on the feet that were pierced for you.

Have you emptied all of your hopes before Him? Then linger, as the woman did, to worship Him.

Worship That Heals

This penitent woman may not have known it at the time but her life was being transformed by her sacrificial worship. As she tenderly embraced Jesus' feet, the vapors from the alabaster box were transformed into the sweet incense of costly worship. The woman arose from that experience of worship forever changed. Not only was she born again, so were her dreams.

There is something about volitional worship in the midst of pain that is especially precious to God. Job's first response to the announcement of inexpressible loss was to rend his garment and worship. It was a willful act. Job could not possibly have known it at the time, but that decision to worship in the midst of unspeakable agony was his first seed sown toward full restoration.

David, as well, knew instinctively that the highest response to the announcement of tragedy was to worship. Upon hearing that the infant offspring of his union with Bathsheba had died, he rose from his bed of anguish, washed his face, and worshiped. Here again, seeds of restoration were being planted.

How well I remember the tormenting jeers of hell as I plowed my way into worship on that afternoon of my father's death. How could praises to God be anything but paramount hypocrisy at such a time? Yet I knew that there was incredible therapy in what I was doing. Far from being hypocritical, the willful worship of my sovereign Lord was impeccably genuine. My sacrifice of praise was the faith-filled acknowledgment that, painful circumstances notwithstanding, Jesus does all things well.

A minister friend of mine experienced the death of his wife. For months he felt unspeakable grief. His ministry came to a complete standstill. He could not encourage others, for all of his emotional reserve was harnessed in his personal battle to keep from sinking. One day he made a decision to praise the Lord in the midst of his loss. He shut the door of his study and lifted his hands to heaven. Numbly he said, "Lord, I praise You." His mind mocked him and his emotions protested violently. Yet he continued to offer his sacrifice of praise. The minutes finally ground into an hour. Then two. Still he worshiped. Three hours passed. Suddenly he felt rumblings deep within him. He said it was as if a dam began to burst inside him. Finally the healing wave broke forth in loving fury. His agony, confusion, and heartsickness were swept away in the adoring streams of living water that poured out of him in praise to God.

Your greatest therapy in pain is to connect with heaven. Your sacrifice of praise will ascend as sweet incense before the Lord. And you, like the woman, will leave healed and restored to a new hope.

The Life That Still Can Be

As long as your alabaster box remains unbroken, safely concealed, you will be unable to receive the new hopes God has for you. For the heart is capable of housing only one alabaster box.

Perhaps this is why some who pronounce themselves delivered from their pasts are actually still enslaved. Jesus stood in the temple and read from Isaiah, "The Spirit of the Lord God is upon Me, because the Lord has anointed Me to preach good tidings to the poor; He has sent Me to heal the brokenhearted, to proclaim liberty to the captives . . ." (Isaiah 61:1). Notice that sandwiched between the proclamation of the gospel and the loosing of the captives is the healing of the brokenhearted.

This is not indiscriminate wording; the order is significant. Before you can be delivered permanently from your captivity, your broken heart must be healed. And Jesus has been commissioned and anointed to do just that — for you, right now.

The Lord has an even more precious box of new hopes He is ready to give you. But first, you must surrender your old alabaster box to Him. Break open its contents before Him. Let your ruined hopes ascend as a fragrant incense in worship. And let Him heal your broken heart.

You have given to Jesus the life that really is. You

have poured out before Him the life that might have been. Now you are ready to receive from Him a wonderful new set of dreams — the life that still can be.

9

The College of Disappointments

When my heart is overwhelmed; lead me to the rock that is higher than I (Ps. 61:2).

Martin Luther said, "Affliction is the best book in my library." Next to Holy Scripture it must be the world's greatest book on human behavior. And if affliction is the best book, then the world-renowned College of Disappointments must be the most thorough of all finishing schools. For in this college the sandpaper of disappointment and the white-hot flame of failure hone and melt the student into finished form.

There is no occurrence in the Christian's life that cannot be redeemed by God: "And we know that all things work together for good to those who love God, to those who are the called according to His purpose. For whom He foreknew, He also predestined to be conformed to the image of His Son, that He might be the firstborn among many brethren" (Rom. 8:28-29). God's overarching purpose for all His children is to conform them into the image of His firstborn Son, the Lord Jesus. Using life as an anvil He takes our disappointments as His mallet, and makes sure that each blow shapes us more into the family likeness of His lovely Son.

With such a marvelous purpose canopying our circumstances, our spirits can be at rest in all situations. No wonder Paul could say, "I have learned in whatever state I am, to be content" (Phil. 4:11). As my dear friend Paul Billheimer said, we are destined for the throne. Our future is to rule and reign with Christ. Our destiny is to be like Him. "Beloved, now we are children of God; and it has not yet been revealed what we shall be, but we know that when He is revealed, we shall be like Him, for we shall see Him as He is. And everyone who has this hope in Him purifies himself, just as He is pure" (1 John 3:2-3).

Did you know that you are becoming like the God you worship? Consider this. Millions the world over worship gods of wood and stone. Those gods cannot hear; they cannot perceive. And many of those imprisoned by such a religion become like the false gods they worship: dull, indifferent, impotent. Then consider the millions of religious zealots in the Middle East. They perceive the almighty as wrathful, vengeful, militant. While they feel he may on occasion show mercy, he would seldom, if ever, show love. And these militaristic, religious devotees are becoming like their concept of the god they worship.

As Christians we too are destined to become like the One we adore. As our eyes are riveted on Jesus, we are being transformed into His likeness "from glory to glory, just as by the Spirit of the Lord" (2 Cor. 3:18). Our destiny is Christlikeness.

Nietzsche, the famed philosopher, said, "He who knows why can endure any how." The "how" of your journey through life is not of final importance, even if you major in suffering in the College of Disappointments. What is of ultimate importance is the "why" of suffering. And the "why" is simply this: "If we endure, we shall also reign with Him" (2 Tim. 2:12).

"God Is Making You Now"

Perhaps at this moment you are in the crucible of suffering. That is where the Refiner's fire burns most fiercely, burning away all that is impure or non-essential.

The story is told of a young mother who had to witness the agony of watching both of her young children fall victim to a monstrous plague. In one day both of her offspring died. She was hysterical with grief and she blurted out through her tears, "I don't see why God made me!"

Her aunt, a wise Christian of many years, comforted her. "Dear," she said, "you are not yet made. God is making you now."

Have such agonies raced through your mind? Do you question why you have had to suffer so? Remember, He's making you now. Submit to the Refiner's fire. Don't waste your sorrows.

A goldsmith was once asked how he checked the purity of his precious metal. He looked down at the liquid gold in the crucible. "When I can see my face in it," he replied, "then it is pure." When our divine Refiner can see His image in us, then we have indeed been purified. And thus purified, we will feel that each degree of heat was worth it.

The classic hymn "How Firm a Foundation" says it so well. Two of the following three stanzas are omitted from many modern hymnals, yet they yield immense, contemporary comfort to those harassed by fiery trials:

> *In every condition, in sickness, in health,*
> *In poverty's vale, or abounding in wealth;*
> *At home and abroad, on the land, on the sea,*
> *As thy days may demand, shall thy strength ever be!*
>
> *When through the deep waters I call thee to go,*
> *The rivers of woe shall not thee overflow;*
> *For I will be with thee, thy troubles to bless,*
> *And sanctify to thee thy deepest distress.*

When through fiery trials thy pathway shall lie,
My grace, all sufficient, shall be thy supply;
The flame shall not hurt thee; I only design
Thy dross to consume, and thy gold to refine.[1]

David's Response or Saul's?

Almost everyone takes a course or two in the College of Disappointments. Not all graduate, however, for the requirements are quite demanding.

Kings Saul and David both experienced disappointment, failure, and rejection. David passed his courses; Saul did not. Many would consider David's sin more costly than Saul's. Yet David died in honor; Saul, a demented man, committed suicide. Both experienced suffering. Both made tragic mistakes. What then made the difference in their lives? Once more we must address the matter of bitterness.

After David was confronted with his transgression — adultery and murder — he fully acknowledged it. He came before the Lord in deep remorse and gave a full accounting. "Against You, You only, have I sinned, and done this evil in Your sight" (Ps. 51:4). He pleaded with God for His continued presence and for the restoration of joy. "Do not cast me away from Your presence, and do not take Your Holy Spirit from me. Restore to me the joy of Your salvation, and uphold me by Your generous Spirit" (Ps. 51:11-12).

Saul started his career with simple trust in the Lord. That changed as power began to corrupt him. He soon saw himself as an exception to the standards of obedience required of the rest of the nation and distanced himself, first from his people, and then from his God.

His partial obedience became so habitual that eventually he actually believed he was walking in full obedience. At one point when Saul was sent by God to destroy the Amalekites and all their possessions, he kept out the best livestock for himself. Samuel confronted him about this disobedience to the Lord's command , and he replied that he had indeed obeyed the Lord to the letter. Having played such mental gymnastics, it is little wonder that he succumbed to fits of melancholy. God took the throne from him, and instead of going to the Lord penitently for relief from his distress, he consulted a witch. Thus, he opened his life to demonic dementia.

Saul envied young David's growing popularity at his expense. On more than one occasion he sought to kill him. But David honored Saul as "the Lord's anointed," even after God's favor clearly had left him. Saul embraced bitterness — a more deadly action than David's embracing of Bathsheba.

Although the disappointments and reversals of your life may be many, fight bitterness like the killer it is. And resolve, as David did, to be restored to a pure, unhindered walk with the Lord.

Present Grace

Some must wake daily to life's disappointments — physical disorders, forced continued contact with a former spouse, a wheelchair.

While we hear much about exercising faith for a release from such circumstances, we seldom hear about exercising faith in the grace of God present in those circumstances.

Paul, who cast out demons and whose hands were a transmitter for God's healing touch, was no less a person of faith because God sovereignly chose not to remove his thorn in the flesh. Christians have always conjectured what Paul's thorn may have been. It is something of a game for us, but it was no game for the Apostle. And whatever his thorn was, it was something he desperately wished wasn't there. Paul would have much preferred freedom or at least reprieve from this unwelcome, constant companion. God chose, rather, to confer upon Paul His enabling endurance as the thorn jabbed his side.

The Apostle turned this deficit into one of his most powerful assets. "Concerning this thing," Paul said, "I pleaded with the Lord three times that it might depart from me. And He said to me, 'My grace is sufficient for you, for My strength is made perfect in weakness.' Therefore most gladly I will rather boast in my infirmities, that the power of Christ may rest upon me. Therefore I take pleasure in infirmities, in reproaches, in needs, in persecutions, in distresses, for Christ's sake. For when I am weak, then I am strong" (2 Cor. 12:8-10).

The most abhorrent difficulties can be reversed into your most powerful opportunities. The devil is smart, but he is by no means omniscient. He often overplays his hand. Thinking that disappointments will crush us, his schemes are spoiled and the very instrument of pain is transformed by the believer into a sacramental means of grace.

The most abhorrent difficulties can be reversed into your most powerful opportunities. The devil is smart but he is by no means omniscient. He often overplays his hand. Thinking that disappointments will crush us, his schemes are spoiled and the very instrument of pain is transformed by the believer into a sacramental means of grace. Then, even though harassed by messengers of Satan, the believer will sing, "God is our refuge and strength, a very present help in trouble" (Ps. 46:1). This triumphant Christian now knows His God in a new dimension. Not only is He a deliverer *from* trouble; He is a very present help *in* trouble.

The Crippled Prince

It is probable that Paul's thorn permanently altered him just as Jacob's wrestling with an angel afflicted him.

The Lord was changing Jacob from a deceptive schemer into a prince with God, but not without struggle. And not without a token of the struggle.

Just before dawn, as the angel pulled away from Jacob and pronounced heaven's blessing on him, God's messenger "touched the socket of his hip" (Gen. 32:25). Consequently, Jacob limped for the rest of his life. He came away from the battle victorious but crippled. He had entered into a new dimension of spiritual authority and blessing, but it had been at the expense of his human ability.

Jacob, his arrogance fully subdued, would go through the rest of his life with incredible spiritual dynamism but he would also have to lean on something stronger. Now he was a walking exhibit of weakness and dependency. Whereas once he rested fully on his own resources, now his physically crippled body portrayed his dependent spirit. He had become the crippled prince.

Has your struggle debilitated you? If you respond correctly, your "limp" can be a token of new dependency coupled with new authority. Isaiah 33:23 says, "The lame take the prey." Satan's schemes have backfired. He has not been able to spoil you. Instead, though limping, you have taken the spoil.

A Door of Hope

Hosea 2:15 describes the Valley of Achor as a door of hope. The word *Achor* means "tears." If, like Paul, God has indicated to you that your suffering will not be relieved this side of heaven, then know that in the lonely valley of tears, God has ordained a door of hope. The pain has been conceived in hell, but God is spoiling Satan's designs. The crippling experience is being masterminded by heaven to thrust you into a realm of princely authority.

10

The Sanctity of Brokenness

That I may know Him and the power of His resurrection, and the fellowship of His sufferings, being conformed to His death (Phil. 3:10).

Why do the righteous suffer?" This age-old query has no simple answer. In fact, at first glance suffering seems to be in contradiction to many of God's promises of blessings for the righteous. If one sows what is just and good, why should he reap disappointment and failure?

It seems that until recently the desire to make some sense out of sorrow was a predominant theme in Christian teaching. Somewhere, several years back, we turned a corner theologically and opted for an "up" gospel. We told our people that they could achieve or obtain anything — *anything* — provided they had the right frame of mind and a happy heart. You must understand that, even as I write this, I am trying to take us on a trip through a morass of issues. I'm not against optimism. I am *not* championing morbidity. But I do get a little squeamish inside when I hear "happiness" being touted as the essence of the Christian message.

I've often wondered what the response of John Wesley or A. W. Tozer would be to some of our current thinking and practices. If they came back for a week and flipped through our Christian magazines, observed our television ministries, attended our concerts and our churches, what would they think? Would they view our faith as only related by marriage (to Jesus) to the faith they embraced? And might they view us not so much as brothers and sisters but as distant cousins to New Testament believers?

We are living in the midst of a spiritual anomaly. On the one hand we are witnessing a powerful spiritual renewal. Yet, on the other hand, the renewal's longevity is being threatened by doctrinal distortions.

The New-Time Gospel

Christians have always cherished what some call the "old-time gospel," the biblical *kerygma* — the proclamation of salvation through Jesus Christ. But today this central message is often taking a back seat to our "relevant" postulations on "Bible-based carefree living." Our new emphasis often seems only slightly connected to our historic faith, a sort of "new-time" gospel.

According to Scripture, suffering is part of the package of being a follower of Jesus. While it is certainly not to be courted, neither is it to be feared. Nor are we necessarily to think of suffering or disappointment as the consequence of a lack of faith. It is clear that one may indeed suffer, not because he has done evil, but because he has done good. Jesus, of course, is the most obvious example. The Bible says that His life was one continuous saga of "going about doing good" (Acts 10:38), yet no one suffered as He did. It is quite possible that some whose eyes He had opened, whose hunger He had fed, whose children He had blessed, were among the mutinous crowd that lobbied in anger for His crucifixion.

Not only is Jesus our example in suffering, He is our example in responding to suffering. Peter speaks powerfully about this point urging that if we do suffer, we should suffer because of what we have done right, not because of what we have done wrong. "For [suffering] is commendable, if because of conscience toward God one endures grief, suffering wrongfully. For what credit is it if, when you are beaten for your faults, you take it patiently? But when you do good and suffer, if you take it patiently, this is commendable before God. For to this you were called, because Christ also suffered for us, leaving us an example, that you should follow His steps: 'Who committed no sin, nor was deceit found in His mouth'; who, when He was reviled, did not revile in return; when He suffered, He did not threaten, but committed himself to Him who judges righteously" (1 Pet. 2:19-23). Peter reminds us that Jesus has left us a sterling example to follow. Not only will we, as His followers, sometimes be called upon to suffer wrongfully, but we are also impelled to respond to such suffering as He responded.

Today's pulpits are transmitting conflicting signals on how to respond to suffering and loss. Some would urge us simply to capitulate to suffering, no questions asked. Others would challenge us to "confess" our way out of such difficulties by positive verbal affirmations. Still others would have us ignore such trials as incongruous with the "overcoming life" that, supposedly, is stress-free. Then there are those who would castigate us for suffering in the first place. "Shame on you," they seem to say, "for not having enough faith to stay out of trouble!"

Yet the sensitive Christian knows that none of these preachments fully meets him in his agony. They are often the distanced replies of those who would have us believe they are unscathed by pain. How different from the empathy of our Lord Jesus, a faithful High Priest, who is touched with the feeling of our weaknesses and tempted in every point as we are (see Heb. 4:15).

Our contemporary answers to suffering bear little resemblance to the historic posture of our Christian predecessors. They viewed suffering as the instrument by which they were progressively being conformed into the likeness of their Saviour, a character development necessary to their future roles of ruling and reigning with Christ. This concept seems only faintly important to many of us today. This is because we have been victimized, in my opinion, by an existentialized Christianity. Such a faith gives heavy emphasis to the immediacy of God's blessings and provision (which I also endorse) but little attention to our future position as the bride of Christ, ruling with Him over the nations. We love to speak of prosperity but often fail to speak of purity. We speak in terms of self-actualization instead of self-denial. We teach on our authority but seldom on posturing ourselves as servants.

Much of our current emphasis is good. Indeed it is a correction to some of our distorted, gloomy perspectives of the past. Yet we are notorious for "pendulum swinging." We seem to think that the only way to correct past errors is by swinging excessively to the other side. These days call for steady, balanced faith and living. The Church must cease its dizzy ride from one pole to the other and finally "land" in a solid central stance.

So, while I find little to disagree with in much current teaching on faith, victory, and prosperity, my concern is with what is being left unsaid. And isn't that what turns a "truth" into a "half-truth?" I may indeed be telling you the truth that there's a pot of gold at the end of the rainbow, but I have done you a terrible disservice if I fail to advise you of the dragons you will have to fight to get there. It is true that there is a faith that delivers from pain and suffering. What is too often left unsaid is that there is also a gallant faith that can only be expressed in suffering.

In fact, Hebrews 11, the Bible chapter listing the great

champions of faith, puts tortured and martyred Christians in the same category as those who subdued kingdoms, escaped the edge of the sword, and stopped the mouths of lions: "And all these . . . obtained a good testimony through faith" (Heb. 11:39).

I see five serious omissions in the new-time gospel, key components of the Christian faith that are being de-emphasized or overlooked.

First, the new-time gospel de-emphasizes suffering. Our seminaries train our ministers in marketing skills and group management. When we speak of "church growth" we immediately think in terms of volume of people and fiscal strength; we seldom perceive "church growth" to be a corporate advance in Christlikeness with its attendant struggles. So in an era of exponential curves, the message of struggle, loss, and suffering is clearly out of vogue. Yet Paul says flatly, "For to you it has been granted on behalf of Christ, not only to believe in Him, but also to suffer for His sake" (Phil. 1:29).

Second, the new-time gospel de-emphasizes sacrifice. The heroic stories of laying aside fortunes for missionary work, of investing one's life in a remote jungle habitation, sound almost senseless to many today. "What's the point?" we seem to ask with a chuckle. We have stressed the fact that "Jesus died to give us the good life" — and left it there. We inferred that the "good life" was based on material possessions. While Christians in the past measured their success by the strength of their piety, we often measure our success by the strength of our pocketbooks.

Again, I need to stress that I am not against material prosperity. Just look at history. Wherever the gospel has dominated, there has inevitably been attendant upward mobility. Poverty is a blight. It is demeaning and dehumanizing to have insufficient money to pay one's bills, to respond to the heart's promptings to give, or to invest for the future. Further, the church must prosper so she will be capable financially of fulfilling her mandate of world evangelization.

The Bible is not against having riches; it is against hoarding riches. For you, as a Christian, it is not inordinate to expect a dependable car, a comfortable home, and financial security for your family. It is, however, not only inordinate but immoral to develop a ravenous lust for "more" because you have been convinced that life does indeed consist in the abundance of things that a person possesses.

This is in polar antithesis to the teaching of Jesus. Jesus said, "Do not lay up for yourselves treasures on earth, where moth and rust destroy and where thieves break in and steal; but lay up for yourselves treasures in heaven, where neither moth nor rust destroys and where thieves do not break in and steal. For where your treasure is, there your heart will be also" (Matt. 6:19-21). Contemporary Christians often have little interest in the hereafter, and Jesus tells us why: They have invested little or no treasure in heaven.

Voluntary sacrifice, like involuntary suffering, makes little sense without an eternal perspective.

Third, the new-time gospel de-emphasizes sin. We are prone today to view sin as an aberration of personality rather than willful transgression. It is true that, on careful scrutiny, one can find inexcusable blunders and volitional indiscretions in each era of the Church's history. Current Christians, however, may have the dubious distinction of taking sin more lightly than any previous generation. Earlier eras emphasized sin to the exclusion of grace, but we have taken a pendulum ride. We often emphasize grace to the exclusion of the seriousness of sin. We need to be reminded again of Deitrich Bonhoeffer's warning, "While God's grace is free, it is not cheap."

Fourth, it is easy to see, then, why the new-time gospel would also de-emphasize sanctification. If we are weak on the consequences of sin, we will certainly be weak on the need for purity. Again, our de-emphasis may have been to correct an earlier distortion. Christian piety has often expressed itself in an embarrassing and unscriptural holier-than-thou-ism. That is seldom our problem today. Today we seem to express little holiness at all! The biblical concept of sanctification means to be set apart for God's intended purpose. It is clearly time to issue a fresh call to such genuine sanctification. It is time for Christians to break free of polluting flirtations and be set apart solely for God's purpose for them.

Finally, the new-time gospel sadly de-emphasizes the second coming of Jesus Christ. We talk primarily in terms of immediacy. "My blessings now" seems to have unseated "Jesus is coming" as our watchword. But Scripture teaches us that we must view this life in the light of Christ's return and the establishment of His kingdom.

Writing the church at Corinth, Paul reminded the believers, who seemed infatuated with temporal sensuality, "If in this life only we have hope in Christ, we are of all men the most pitiable" (1 Cor. 15:19). He also told them, "For our light affliction, which is but for a moment, is working for us a far more exceeding and eternal weight of glory, while we do not look at the things which are seen, but at the things which are not seen. For the things which are seen are temporary, but the things which are not seen are eternal" (2 Cor. 4:17-18).

Peter stressed the eternal dimension: "Beloved, do not think it strange concerning the fiery trial which is to try you, as though some strange thing happened to you; but rejoice to the extent that you partake of Christ's sufferings, that when His glory is revealed, you may also be glad with exceeding joy" (1 Pet. 4:12-13). He also encouraged believers to remember that they had "an inheritance incorruptible and undefiled and that does not fade away, reserved in heaven for you" (1 Pet. 1:4).

John includes his voice in the swell of encouragement to look for the return of Christ. "And now, little children, abide in Him, that when He appears, we may have confidence and not be ashamed before Him at His coming" (1 John 2:28).

Then, of course, there is the tender encouragement of Jesus himself to keep our hearts riveted toward heaven. "In My Father's house are many mansions; if it were not so, I would have told you. I go to prepare a place for you. And if I go and prepare a place for you, I will come again and receive you to Myself; that where I am, there you may be also" (John 14:2-3).

When we consider our sufferings alongside Christ's return, then they can be viewed as lovingly orchestrated opportunities for growth for our future rulership with Him. Paul Billheimer speaks pointedly to this:

> The center of gravity of God's discipline is not time but eternity. Allowing God's discipline to wean one from vain ambition and selfishness increases agape love and transmutes one's brokenness into eternal glory. Rejecting and refusing the painful circumstances which God planned should crucify all the life of nature and of self is to waste one's sorrows.
>
> All the unspeakable suffering of the saints, the combined sorrows, tragedies, heartaches, disappointments, the persecutions and martyrdoms in the history of the Church Universal from the first century to this present throbbing moment, all of these can be justified only by taking eternity into consideration. All of them serve a purpose in the here and now, but their principle design is to teach agape love in preparation for eternal rulership. Suffering is God's grand strategy for creating rank in the Bridehood for His eternal enterprise. It seems that only this can possibly justify earth's flood of sorrow.[1]

The Jesus Touch

So it seems clear that the ultimate rationale for the believer's being allowed to suffer is to knead into his character the Christlike love that will be necessary for his rulership with Christ. But, in the meantime, there is tremendous benefit in this life as well. Suffering allows us not merely to sympathize but to empathize with others facing difficulty. Through suffering we enter a realm of brokenness whereby the mercy of Jesus pours out of us. I call it "the Jesus touch."

The Bible says that Jesus was a "Man of sorrows and acquainted with grief" (Isa. 53:3). When Jesus took on humanness, He voluntarily forfeited several divine prerogatives. Although He was God as well as a man, He allowed himself to experience human emotions and deprivations. He sorrowed. He wept. He needed sleep. He rejoiced. He was thirsty. He was hungry. He was rejected. He was murdered. He allowed himself to experience the gamut of human joy and pain, while remaining "holy, harmless, undefiled, separate from sinners" (Heb. 7:26).

Why did He choose to suffer, when suffering could have been avoided? Hebrews 2:17-18 gives the answer: "And it was necessary for Jesus to be like us, his brothers, so that he could be our merciful and faithful High Priest before God, a Priest who would be both merciful to us and faithful to God in dealing with the sins of the people. For since he himself has now been through suffering and temptation, he knows what it is like when we suffer and are tempted, and he is wonderfully able to help us" (Heb. 2:17-18;LB). As Alexander Maclaren, the noted Scottish preacher, said, "The hands that were pierced do move the wheels of human history and mold the circumstances of individual lives."

If we refuse to become embittered, we can tie our suffering to His, thus allowing His touch to be extended through ours. I once viewed brokenness as important for effective ministry. Now I consider it mandatory. It must be remembered that we cannot engineer the circumstances of our personal Calvary; we cannot predetermine the events that will produce personal brokenness. Certainly it would be unhealthy to seek such an experience, but tragedy, if it does occur, can be the instrument of crucifixion for our own arrogance and independence.

It is vital to keep our eyes on Jesus, not only during the crisis, but after the crisis as well. For even if we respond well during the fiery trial, we may be prone to bitterness afterward. If that happens the positive effects of the brokenness have been aborted. As Dr. Billheimer has conjectured, "One is not broken until all resentment and rebellion against God and man is removed."

Without the Jesus touch on one's life, even high visibility and plenty of accolades are a grief to the spirit.

The Fellowship of His Sufferings

The apostle Paul thrived on intimacy with Jesus. The visible confrontation with Christ on the Damascus road did something to Paul that forever altered him. Having seen the Lord, he would never be content with a frothy, surface relationship with Him. Paul wrote of his desire for intimacy with Jesus in Philippians 3:10: "That I may know Him and the power of His resurrection, and the fellowship of His sufferings, being conformed to His death."

Most of us, with Paul, want to know Jesus "and the power of His resurrection." Far fewer wish to progress to the second level of intimacy: the fellowship of His sufferings, even being conformed to His death. Yet there is a dimension of richness in such intimacy that profoundly affects all who are touched by such a life. When one experiences intense disappointment, it becomes a springboard to increased fellowship with Jesus himself. For as long as hopes and dreams are central, it is easy (if not inevitable) for us to be consumed with goals instead of God, with Christian things instead of Christ himself. But when dreams lie in ruins at our feet, then we focus once more on what is of ultimate importance. We see afresh our need for that which endures; our need for friendships, our need for God, and, most importantly, our need for friendship with God.

So lost dreams often become the springboard to the fellowship of His sufferings. The entrance requirements into this esteemed fellowship are high indeed. But the benefits are lifelong. For when the tide turns again (as surely it will) you will have a depth and richness that could never have been there otherwise. There is gain in loss. And disappointment is not an exercise in futility if the disappointment is the doorway to richer communion with Jesus Christ. In that place of intimacy, even the pain becomes precious as the Lord becomes the Balm of Gilead for your wounds and as your tears become the water with which you wash His pierced feet.

When our faith has taken us to the very precipice of endurance, when for inexplicable reasons our hopes have been shot down, then we really learn to trust God — not just His promises, but Him.

No doubt the unknown poet was thinking of these rich dividends to suffering when he or she wrote:

> *Measure thy life by loss and not by gain*
> *Not by the wine drunk, but by the wine poured forth.*
> *For love's strength standeth in love's sacrifice,*
> *And he who suffers most has most to give.*

When our faith has taken us to the very precipice of endurance, when for inexplicable reasons our hopes have been shot down, then we really learn to trust God — not just His promises, but Him.

The Bible recounts the tragedy of a king's hopes that were severely crushed. Good King Jehoshaphat did what was right in the eyes of the Lord according to Scripture. He conducted a moral clean-up campaign throughout Judah and modeled godly leadership. Further, promoting unity, he sought and made peace with the king of Israel. No doubt his ambition to commission ships for gold from Ophir was in the interest of his nation. Jehoshaphat was known for his impeccable integrity. Now his noble scheme to bolster his nation's economy was ready for christening.

But something went wrong. "Jehoshaphat made merchant ships to go to Ophir for gold; but they never sailed, for the ships were wrecked at Ezion Geber" (1 Kings 22:48).

Have there been some boats filled with dreams in your life that, though set to sail for gold, were wrecked instead on some rocky coast? "Why?" is the first question blurted out by your heart. What whim of sovereignty allows some ships to return, laden with riches from Ophir, while others are crushed before they ever set sail?

Sometimes all we can do is cling to the fact that even in the wake of wrecked vessels, the Jesus touch and the fellowship of His sufferings are ever more deeply embedded in our hearts. These words of an unknown poet express it well:

> *I will not doubt, though all my ships at sea*
> *Come drifting home with broken masts and sails;*
> *I will believe the hand which never fails*
> *From seeing evil worketh good for me.*
> *And though I weep because those sails are tattered,*
> *Still will I cry, while my best hopes lie shattered:*
> *"I trust in Thee."*

It seems that the "fate," so to speak, of those who would be used of God is to be tutored through some experience of brokenness. Great sainthood, for whatever reasons, often means great suffering. The Psalmist said, "It is good for me that I have been afflicted, that I may learn Your statutes" (Ps. 119:71). Paul said, "We also glory in tribulations, knowing that tribulation produces perseverance; and perseverance, character; and character, hope" (Rom. 5:3-4). Far from being a destroyer of hope, tribulations can actually entrench hope in the heart of the one schooled by difficulties.

Wholeness via Brokenness

Sometimes God allows our dreams to be destroyed, not because they are too big but because they are too small. He desires even greater things for us than we can yet imagine. Often there must be a deeper working of His life in us before we are able to sustain the greater vision He wishes to bestow. Thus, we are allowed a period of suffering. If brokenness ensues from unrealized hopes of the past, then we can receive an even greater vision for the future.

God desires to thrust us into an other-worldly dimension of His blessing. But first, all arrogance must be removed. We must learn how dependent we are on Him *before* we see our dreams come true. Else we would become like the Israelites who mistakenly supposed that their own ingenuity was the cause of their blessings. In fact, God allowed the Israelites to go through an actual wilderness experience to wean them from their haughtiness: "... that He might humble you and that He might test you, to do you good in the end — [lest] you say in your heart, 'My power and the might of my hand have gained me this wealth' " (Deut. 8:16-17).

Do you see it? God allowed the Israelites to go through the wilderness to work humility into them so they might praise the proper Source of their blessings. Also, even though they were humbled and tested, it was for God's expressed purpose "to do you good in the end." The measure of your life's success is not in where you are when you start out, but where you are when you end up. For most of the enslaved Israelites, their highest goal was freedom from the Egyptian oppressors. But as they trudged through endless miles of desert, God birthed in them a far loftier vision than a quick exit out of Egypt. They were to be a model nation, declaring His glory among the nations.

Your original dream, though precious to you, may have been too small for God. Now in the scorching heat of trial, an even greater hope is being born. And this time it is completely free of self-exaltation. When this dream comes to pass, "you shall remember the Lord your God, for it is He who gives you power to get wealth, that He may establish His covenant which He swore to your fathers" (Deut. 8:18). "Blessed are the poor in spirit," Jesus said, "for theirs is the kingdom of heaven" (Matt. 5:3). In other words, blessed are those who realize their total dependency on God. They will realize heaven's possibilities.

In the early days of the ministry of radio pioneer Charles E. Fuller, pressure over needed finances and stress from constant travel crippled him to the point of emotional collapse. It was a crushing weight. But a few months afterward, Fuller was back, with more anointing and greater empathy than ever. It was as if his dream rose out of the ashes to far greater heights. His "Old-Fashioned Revival Hour" was broadcast weekly to more than twenty million listeners, an audience greater than any of the mega television ministries of our day. And this happened at a time when America's population was far less. One can only imagine the immense impact of such a ministry in the midst of a war-torn nation. Today, the seminary he founded, Fuller Theological Seminary, and its School of World Mission carry on the global vision of a broken yet powerful man.

Charles H. Spurgeon sank into deep depression after a tragedy that was supposed to be a triumph. One of England's largest auditoriums was jammed with people eager to hear the young Baptist preacher. But a shout of "Fire!" caused a stampede as people trampled one another to escape. Several were crushed to death. Spurgeon never fully recovered from the shock and fits of despondency that followed him throughout his life. But he would rise above the agony. He would build London's greatest church. And today he is considered by many to be the greatest preacher since the fourth century Chrysostom.

Little did Bob Pierce know the immense cost involved in the fulfillment of his prayer, "Let my heart be broken by the things that break the heart of God." He wept his way home from the aftermath of the Korean War, where he had witnessed unclaimed children eating out of trash cans and sleeping under cardboard. Pierce's life would be blasted by personal and professional tragedies. But he left behind two great Christian humanitarian ministries, World Vision and Samaritan's Purse. They were born, as one friend said, not so much as organizations but as the spurting blood from Pierce's broken heart.

A dream that doesn't cost anything isn't worth the effort. But these lives give ample evidence that you, too, can rise above your present heartache to greater heights than ever before. Your sufferings are doing something to you or for you. Which will it be? Let there be a sanctity in your brokenness. Let it work for your greater character, greater potential, and, eventually, greater glory. "For I consider that the sufferings of this present time are not worthy to be compared with the glory which shall be revealed in us" (Rom. 8:18).

11

Leave a Well

Who passing through the valley of Baca make it
a well; the rain also filleth the pools (Ps. 84:6;KJV).

One day I was browsing in a Christian bookstore's music section, and noticed an album that had been produced by a college friend of mine, Neal Joseph. It was Gordon Jensen's *Gallery*, which included his beautiful song "Leave a Well in the Valley."

To the valley you've been through
Those around you must go too.
Down the rocky path you've traveled
They will go.
If, to those learning of your trial,
You'll lend the secret of your smile,
You will help them more than you will ever know.

Blessed is the man
Who has learned to understand,
To become a hand for God
To those in need.

Then all the tears you've shed,
With God's help they become instead
A precious balm that will heal hearts that bleed.

Leave a well in the valley,
Your dark and lonesome valley,
Because others have to walk that valley too.
What a blessing when they find
The well of joy you've left behind,
Leave a well in the valley you go through.[1]

Even in the desert experiences of our lives, there is an oasis. In the middle of seemingly God-forsaken hothouses of trouble, Jesus is still the Living Water. The Bible says, "For waters shall burst forth in the wilderness, and streams in the desert. The parched ground shall become a pool, and the thirsty land springs of water" (Isa. 35:6-7). If God has allowed you to trudge through some parched desert, you may be sure that He has also prepared an underground artesian spring to refresh you. But you will have to dig to discover it!

Digging Deep for Future Travelers

The Bible says that the Holy Spirit led Jesus into the wilderness. This means there was a God-ordained, prepared wilderness experience for the Lord. There may be a God-ordained wilderness for you as well. Just remember that, though God may have had a hand in allowing you to be in the desert, it is certainly not His intention that you die there. So, along your path, He has placed some underground streams.

You see, when everything is going well, your needs can be quenched on the surface. But when you're in the desert, your thirst can only be quenched by digging deep. And you needn't fear that it will be a dry well; the river is there. "There is a river whose streams shall make glad the city of God" (Ps. 46:4). There's a prepared place of nourishment and refreshment for you, just as surely as there's a prepared wilderness experience.

In the midst of your trial, God wants to reveal himself to you in a greater dimension than ever before. He wants to be unveiled to you as the God of all comfort. "Blessed be the God and Father of our Lord Jesus Christ, the Father of mercies and God of all comfort, who comforts us in all our tribulation, that we may be able to comfort those who are in any trouble, with the comfort with which we ourselves are comforted by God. For as the sufferings of Christ abound in us, so our consolation also abounds through Christ" (2 Cor. 1:3-5).

Many who know God in dimensions of salvation and even discipleship have yet to know Him as Comforter. This is the very title Jesus gave to the Holy Spirit whom He said He would bequeath to the Church. The Authorized Version of the Bible records Jesus as encouraging his bewildered disciples, "And I will pray the Father, and he shall give you another Comforter, that he may abide with you for ever; even the Spirit of truth... But the Comforter, which is the Holy Ghost, whom the Father will send in my name, he shall teach you all things" (John 14:16-17,26). Notice too that Jesus said, "I will not leave you comfortless: I will come to you" (John 14:18).

We're talking about inner refreshment in the midst of hot difficulties. Jesus can become more precious to you at such times than He ever was previously. He has promised not to orphan or abandon us. Remember He said, "I will never leave you nor forsake you" (Heb. 13:5). Here He lovingly encourages His followers: "In a way I'm leaving, yet in another way I'll always be with you. I won't leave you victimized by the scorching elements of trouble. I'll ask the Father and He will send you a Comforter. In fact, the Comforter will actually be Me, simply in another form. I will come to you."

The Holy Spirit is the expression of Jesus to us today. Between Christ's physical ascension into heaven and His personal return to earth one day, He inhabits this planet and His people by His Spirit — the Holy Spirit.

Tragically, many Christians know little about the Holy Spirit. Perhaps one reason is that, on the mountaintop, "Christian work" can often be achieved merely by our noble efforts, though such ministry may have very little lasting effect. But in the desert all human resources are depleted, leaving us parched. And it is there that God promises streams in the desert. It is there that Jesus says, "I will come to you." And He comes in the Person of the Holy Spirit.

> *One great benefit of wilderness traveling is that it produces thirst. You probably picked up this book because you're in some desert. Are you thirsty? I have wonderful news for you. There's plenty of water — if only you know where to dig.*

After some time has elapsed in the desert, we become desperate. We start to dig inner wells, exploring that which has heretofore been capped over, for whatever reasons. As we begin to dig for these inner springs, we discover, usually to our astonishment, that there's plenty of cold, refreshing water down there. How did we go so long without making this fantastic discovery of an inner artesian well! The answer is clear: Before we were in the desert, we were never sufficiently thirsty. Jesus said, "Blessed are those who hunger and thirst for righteousness, for they shall be filled" (Matt. 5:6). The primary requirement for spiritual satiation is hunger and thirst.

One great benefit of wilderness traveling is that it produces thirst. You probably picked up this book because you're in some desert. Are you thirsty? I have wonderful news for you. There's plenty of water — if only you know where to dig.

I remember some time back coming into the house after jogging in the hot Texas sun. I was drenched with perspiration, my face was beet red, and my tongue was thick and dry. I searched quickly for anything that would assuage my craving for something cold and refreshing. I threw open the refrigerator and saw a bottle of ice-cold orange soda. Hurriedly I unscrewed the top and gulped down the entire bottle. Did that taste good! — for about a minute. Suddenly I realized that my thirst had returned, more violently this time. My mouth felt even dryer and thicker. And it was compounded by a sticky, syrupy taste that threatened to clamp my tongue to my palate.

At that moment, I realized that what I needed was not orange soda. I needed water. If you're agonizing with thirst, don't be fooled by substitutes. What you need is water. Jesus said, "If anyone thirsts, let him come to Me and drink. He who believes in Me, as the Scripture has said, out of his heart will flow rivers of living water" (John 7:37-38).

What an invitation! And what a promise! Don't get thrown off track. The surface stuff will not satisfy. Sometimes we look for refreshment in every direction except where the water is. Seminars are good. Books and tapes are fine. But they're only to be used as treasure maps to point you to the water.

Are you thirsty? Then go to Jesus and drink. And drink. And drink. There's ample comfort and refreshment in Him. Soon you will be so full of His Spirit that you will discover that the water is no longer being poured into you. It's being poured out from you because there are lots of others around that are just as thirsty as you were.

Dare to uncap those deep wells. After all, you have only two options: get to the water or die in the wilderness. The Bible says that Jesus was led *by the Spirit* into the wilderness. And after His triumph over the devil there, He was then brought out *by the Spirit* in anointing and power. So don't see your wilderness only as the devil's doing. It may well be that you have been led there by the

Spirit, so that you may learn where the deep, satisfying wells of life can be found. And you will find that this river of life, which flows from the Garden of Eden to the throne of God in the heavenly city, is now tunneling its way through you.

Are you thirsty? Then drink from the clear, eternal streams of the Spirit of the living Christ. For the rivers of living water of which Jesus spoke are, in fact, the artesian gushings of the Holy Spirit. "But this [message about rivers of living water] He spoke concerning the Spirit, whom those believing in Him would receive; for the Holy Spirit was not yet given, because Jesus was not yet glorified" (John 7:39). But now Jesus has been glorified. The Holy Spirit has been given. So don't cap over the wells of living water in you. Don't dam up the flow. Break open those seals. Let the dam burst. There's water down there. Let it rush out over your parched soul.

As you find yourself being sustained by the wells, you will see more reasons for digging them. First, as Gordon Jensen said, others will be coming through this valley. They, too, will need to find water. So leave a well where they can drink — and perhaps some kind of map.

There's one more very good reason to dig this deep well now: Somewhere down the line, you'll be back. And when you travel once again through this valley that seems strangely familiar, you'll know where the water is.

The Well of Tenderness

As you bore deeply, allow the Holy Spirit to construct a well of tenderness through which He can flow. We seem to be reentering an age of barbarism. Little kindnesses, assumed a few years ago, are rare novelties today. Even among Christians, our manners toward one another are often coarse and crude. In short, there is a desperate need today for us to re-dig the wells of tenderness and kindness.

Jesus warned of a time when epidemic crime would

choke out mercy. "And because lawlessness will abound, the love of many will grow cold" (Matt. 24:12). But no matter how the general populace reacts, Christians are enjoined to love one another with a pure heart, fervently. We are called upon to "do good to all, especially to those who are of the household of faith" (Gal. 6:10).

People never forget kindness, especially in a time of crisis. I remember a few years ago visiting Westminster Hall, the great Methodist edifice in central London. This beautiful old structure was turned into a bomb shelter during World War II. For many harrowing nights the gallant pastor of the church, W. E. Sangster, ministered to the frightened masses who crowded into the underground halls. On Sundays he would preach in the upstairs auditorium, which seats some three thousand.

Now, years after Sangster's death, I was walking through the building, admiring a life-sized statue of John Wesley and drinking in the history of the place. I noticed a little book stall in the corner of the main lobby, and behind the stall was a pleasant little man. His plaid shirt was graced by a tie that must have been a good six inches wide. Stuck prominently on the tie was a sticker: "Smile! God loves you."

We chatted for a couple of minutes. Then I remarked, "This is where Sangster pastored, isn't it?"

Immediately a single tear began sliding down the old gentleman's cheek. "You couldn't fit all the people in here in those days," he replied with a faraway gaze. "We'll never forget him."

Your kindness will live longer than you will. And people today are desperate for it. A word. A prayer. A call. A note. A touch. In your own valley of hurt, touch others. Leave a well of tenderness.

Fanny Crosby was asked which of her thousands of stanzas to Christian hymns she considered her best. Pausing to reflect, this little giant of a saint replied, "I think it's this one:"

Down in the human heart,
Crushed by the Tempter,
Feelings lie buried that grace can restore.
Touched by a loving heart, wakened by kindness,
Chords that were broken will vibrate once more.[2]

The Well of Empathy

Our generation seems to have a greater need for counseling than any previous generation. We are desperate to talk to someone about our hurts. I commend every Christian counselor who attempts to help people recover emotionally. The counselor who seeks emotional healing for his patients should be as highly esteemed as the medical doctor who seeks physical healing for his patients. Nevertheless, it remains true that probably the most therapeutic response to someone's hurt is to be able to say, "I understand how you feel. I've been there."

One of the important lasting benefits of your difficulties is empathy. Remember, God comforts us in our present trials so we will later be able to comfort others in similar difficulties.

I have long admired the ministry of Terry Law. I remember as a teenager in high school going to hear this powerful Canadian evangelist. Terry is still preaching. He has had a tremendous effect, particularly in sensitive situations overseas where many would fear to go.

But his life has been marked by tragedy. Preachers in the will of God are not exempt from having their world cave in around them. One night while Terry was in England, preparing to go to Europe, he received a phone call from one of his staff in Tulsa. Terry's wife had just been killed in a car accident.

Terry struggled through the months of ensuing agony by learning to offer God a literal sacrifice of praise. One can never doubt the sovereign love of God in difficult times after hearing his story of how he met the charming woman who is now his wife.

A couple of years after Terry's wife had died, he confided to an associate that he believed he and his children were now ready for him to remarry. The associate prayed for Terry to meet "just the right one." Terry, in his list of "specifications" that he shared with his associate, said he wanted to marry someone who was also widowed so they could appreciate each other's heartache.

One Saturday morning soon after, Terry took his children to McDonald's for breakfast. That act might have been nothing more than a pleasant outing, except the power of God was at work.

Across town a beautiful, godly widow was preparing breakfast for her children. Suddenly she felt strongly impressed to take her two children to McDonald's as her husband used to do. (No doubt some would certainly question that kind of "word" from the Lord!) She had already scrambled the eggs and shook off the impression as a misread signal. But again, she felt strangely urged to leave immediately and head for the golden arches.

"Come on, kids," she said, "we're going out for breakfast."

They dressed quickly, and off they went. Surprisingly, her daughter burst into tears. "This reminds me of Daddy," she said.

At that Shirley almost turned back. But again she was powerfully impressed to keep driving. She prayed with them and her son said, "God's going to give us a new daddy."

Arriving at McDonald's, Shirley saw Terry. Several years earlier her family had hosted members of Terry's singing group, Living Sound, in their home. She went over to his table and asked how those Living Sound singers she had met years ago were doing. As they talked, Terry inquired, "Where does your husband work?"

"Oh, he died some time ago," she replied.

Terry remembers a very strange sensation, both of empathy and growing excitement, surging through him.

To make a wonderful story shorter than it should be, their families have merged and Terry and Shirley are husband and wife.

A chance encounter? Or a loving, sovereign set-up? You be the judge.

Now Terry Law says, "I understand," with authority. His ministry is more effective than ever. I have watched him minister with tremendous compassion. He has been through the crucible of sufferings, and he has seen how God can help the hurting. His life emits empathy. He has left a well.

The Well of Refreshment

Paul Billheimer said, "Only great sufferers are truly benevolent." This is verified by the support groups that have sprouted up around the country. They are usually comprised of people who are either presently sharing a similar pain or who, having come out on the other side, are dipping waters of refreshment to others.

If historians were to summarize our generation, they might well write this epitaph: "They gave up." Thousands in every area of life are bailing out. Runaway children. Runaway fathers and mothers. Workers who one day just don't show up — and never show up again. Suicides. And then there are the millions who are escape artists from life via drugs or alcohol or even nonstop entertainment or seclusion.

Again, the Bible predicted such a time: "Even the youths shall faint and be weary, and the young men shall utterly fall" (Isa. 40:30). Those with a little more chronology under their belts have stopped sighing, "Oh, to be young again." Usually they say, "I'm glad I don't have to face what these kids are up against today."

Billy Graham has said, "This generation is dying not so much from external pressure as from internal combustion." Time and again, the agonized wails of the families of suicide victims cry, "Everything seemed to be okay. He never indicated that he was hurting."

There is a vast need today for experienced travelers who will throw open the floodgates and let their inner resources spill out in refreshment on the weary. The church must return to compassionate evangelism and caring nurture of its own. It is time to lift high the Lord Jesus as the source of life-restoring refreshment and renewal. He specializes in turning bums into responsible husbands and fathers, giving prostitutes a sense of self-worth, and showing hopeless teenagers a reason to wake up in the morning.

In that wonderful few years known as the Jesus movement of the late 1960s and early 1970s, a gentle breeze of God's Spirit blew across this country. During that time a California college football player took particular offense at the happy young Christian who, complete with his guitar, long hair, and sandals, was passing out tracts with a "God bless you!" in front of his fraternity house.

The athlete confronted him. "You guys are so weird. It looks to me like your Jesus takes people and turns them into freaks."

"No, man," the young convert replied. "Jesus takes freaks and turns them into people!"

We need another wind of the Spirit like that to blow on us. It can begin with you. Just dig a well of refreshment for those who want to come and drink.

Your "death valley days" are not permanent. But the wells you dig can be. They can be a source of blessing for today's weary traveler and an oasis for generations to come.

"Therefore with joy you will draw water from the wells of salvation" (Isa. 12:3).

12

Can These Bones Live?

To console those who mourn in Zion, to give them beauty for ashes, the oil of joy for mourning, the garment of praise for the spirit of heaviness; that they may be called trees of righteousness, the planting of the Lord, that He may be glorified (Isa. 61:3).

When the devil, the arch-enemy of Christianity, attacks you, you may be sure he will go for the jugular. Jesus warned, "The thief [the devil] does not come except to steal, and to kill, and to destroy" (John 10:10). So this sinister killer, when he attacks, is not so interested in dealing you a setback as he is in dealing you a knockout punch from which you will never recover.

Faith, Hope, and Love

Satan's master plot is to choke out the very essence of the Christian life. He grips his steely fingers around the three primary components of your faith and begins slowly to choke these life sources. Paul said the three abiding essentials of Christianity are faith, hope, and love. The devil is well aware of the importance of this threefold foundation. So, rather than wasting his time on non-essentials, he blasts his fiery darts at the crux of Christian living.

The devil attacks faith by attempting to make you skeptical. He attacks hope by working to make you cynical. And he attacks love by trying to make you critical. If he succeeds, for all practical purposes, he has you exactly where he wants you — in his corner.

The devices and schemes of the devil are not new. They are tried, time-honored ploys that generally succeed — *unless* you are aware of what he is up to. Concerning these diabolical yet identifiable schemes, Paul said, "We are not ignorant of his [Satan's] devices" (2 Cor. 2:11).

Never forget it: You are most vulnerable when you are discouraged. Your enemy is a soldier who not only plans how he will attack, but when. He waits for a time of apparent weakness, then he comes full force. We must learn then to counter by encouraging ourselves in the Lord. When David was being hunted as prey, the Bible says that he "strengthened himself in the Lord his God" (1 Sam. 30:6). You do the same.

It is when we are susceptible because of discouragement that the devil blasts away at faith, hope, and love, perhaps beginning with faith. If Satan can succeed in eroding your faith, there is no longer any possibility of advancing in your walk with the Lord. The Bible says, "Without faith it is impossible to please Him" (Heb. 11:6). We live in an era of doubt. It seems to hang in the air. Consequently we must build mental reinforcements by daily megadoses of God's Word. "Faith comes by hearing, and hearing by the word of God" (Rom. 10:17). The counter to skepticism is ever-increasing faith. And the pathway to bolster faith is strong familiarity with the Scriptures.

We seem to be living in the age prophesied by these words: "Because lawlessness will abound, the love of many will grow cold" (Matt. 24:12). Just think about it. Twenty-five years ago you probably wouldn't have thought twice about picking up a hitchhiker — it was the courteous thing to do. No more. Fear of "what could happen" floods our minds and counters any inclinations to assist others. Our slogan, at least subconsciously, seems to be, "Don't get involved." Our "bowels of mercies" are clogged with fear, anger, and an overriding concern for self-preservation. This self-preservation fetish causes some to amass personal arsenals against the outside world.

So, the devil capitalizes on this fear. He next attacks love through our growing criticism. The Bible teaches that "love will cover a multitude of sins" (1 Pet. 4:8). How, then, can we recapture lost love? By the Holy Spirit. "The love of God has been poured out in our hearts by the Holy Spirit" (Rom. 5:5). The key to restored faith is large doses of Scripture and the key to restored love is total openness to the Holy Spirit. When the Spirit is allowed to control us, He pushes out all criticism, replacing it with His compassion. We have a supernatural capacity to forgive, to cover another's transgressions, and to care genuinely when we allow the Holy Spirit to control us. "The fruit of the Spirit is love . . ." (Gal. 5:22).

Then there is the issue of hope — the capacity to anticipate the future joyfully. At a casual glance, hope would not seem to be quite as essential as faith or love. Indeed, Paul categorized these three essentials and put love at the top of the list. Without hope, however, faith and love cannot survive. That is why lingering discouragement is so deadly: It makes us cynical, and that destroys our hope.

What is the antidote to cynicism? How can hope be restored? The answer lies in an adjusted perspective. We must learn to focus on what is eternal though invisible. The Bible says that Moses "endured [hoped] as seeing Him who is invisible" (Heb. 11:27). Jesus was able to endure the pain and shame of the cross "for the joy that was set before Him" (Heb. 12:2). When we adjust our perspectives to heaven's values, we are able to begin again, to hope again. That is why Paul encouraged the Colossians, "Set your mind on things above, not on things on the earth" (Col. 3:2).

So remember, the devil will fire away at the core of your life: faith, love, and hope. If you become, as a result, skeptical, critical, and cynical, his scheme has indeed succeeded. How tragic to live — and then to die — faithless, embittered, and without a future. It doesn't matter what the circumstances were that turned a person into a skeptic, or a critic, or a cynic. What matters is that it happened, that he succumbed to the diabolical scheme.

So minimize your vulnerability. Determine by the grace of God not to live in habitual discouragement. Bolster faith by the Word of God. Untap new reservoirs of love by the Holy Spirit. And dare to hope again by a refocused perspective on the things and on the One that can never be taken away from you.

A Monument to Failure

A disillusioned prophet found himself in a valley of despair one day desperately trying to regain his perspective. He, too, had felt the stinging darts of Satan that had punctured his faith, his love, his very hope.

As he viewed the heap of dry bones around him, he saw a literal monument to failure. The dream of victory had been thoroughly squelched in some distant battle. Gallant young soldiers with crisp vision marched to their doom. Now all that was left was a collective monument of the bones of these once-visionary fighters.

Whether Ezekiel's description of this valley of dry bones is literal or figurative is not the issue. He was witnessing, either with his physical or spiritual eyes, a monument to failure. Having been victimized by other disappointments, this horrifying vision was also a vivid reminder of his own dashed, ruined dreams.

There seems to be an almost irrevocable three-stage pattern to God-inspired dreams. First, God plants the vision or dream in the heart. There the dream is allowed to develop and take shape. It is much as if the person carrying the dream were pregnant. The inner, forming "child" of hope becomes deeply cherished, even before birth.

Then, at some point, the vision is "birthed." There's great rejoicing. But quickly something seems to go wrong. Soon it is discovered that the dream is not capable of sustaining life on its own. So the dream is attached to "life-support systems." There's a struggle to keep the dream alive.

Then one day, no matter how much we may protest, the dream dies. Like Ezekiel we stand in a valley of dry bones. His vision was so entirely dead that even the shape of it had vanished. All that was left was a gruesome reminder of what had once been a dream with structure and meaning.

With the death of Ezekiel's vision there was also a death of hope. The prophet was now so demoralized that he dared not believe in a rebirth of the vision. The Spirit of the Lord pointedly asked Ezekiel, "Can these bones live?" No longer was Ezekiel a naive optimist. In utter despair he sighed, "O Lord God, only You know."

But wait. That death of the vision was only the second stage. For those who trust in God, death is never the final chapter. A cornerstone of our faith states, "I believe in the resurrection of the dead." For the believer, there is always a resurrection after death. The second stage must now give way to the third stage: resurrection of the vision.

There are no eternal nights for Christians. As C. S. Lewis said, "Christians never say goodbye." Indeed there are nights of despair, but they are fleeting. There are no eternal nights, but there is an eternal day.

"Can these bones live?" Not only *can* they live. They *must*.

A Framework for Hope

It was at this point the Spirit gave Ezekiel the first of three commands to bring about this resurrection. In the midst of abject discouragement, He commanded him, "Prophesy to the bones." In essence, the Spirit of God was saying, "Command your hopes to come back to life." Nothing around him supported any such encouragement. In fact, Ezekiel must have appeared a perfect fool as he preached resurrection to a heap of bones. But in obedience to the word of the Lord, he commanded the bones — representative of his hopes — to take shape once again.

The Scripture says, "There was a noise, and suddenly a rattling; and the bones came together, bone to bone" (Ezek. 37:7). There was, once again, a connectedness to the long-discarded hopes. This carries the idea of a willingness to re-establish relationships, a daring to dream again and to get involved in life again.

A tragic fallout of discarded dreams is a tendency to reclusiveness. Because of failure we are reluctant to risk again. Because of hurt we are too fearful to trust again. Because of disappointment we are too discouraged to dream again. How, then, do we dare to start over? Because we are commanded to do so by the "loving shove" of God's Spirit.

> *Because of failure we are reluctant to risk again. Because of hurt we are too fearful to trust again. Because of disappointment we are too discouraged to dream again. How, then, do we dare to start over? Because we are commanded to do so by the "loving shove" of God's Spirit.*

This is an important point that must be stressed. Only sovereign intervention can cause your reemerging hopes to take shape once again. It is insufficient simply to "confess it;" God himself must intervene. Herein lies the difficulty of some present teachings on faith: *We are not at liberty to choose the dreams that we wish resurrected.* This is God's prerogative. He alone is in control of the resurrection business.

To try to rebuild our dreams without His directive would only mean, at best, succumbing to the mistakes of the past, and, at worst, resembling the idolmakers Habakkuk described who tried in vain to make their wood and stone creations live. Habakkuk says of them, "Of what value is an idol, since a man has carved it? . . . . For he who makes it trusts in his own creation . . . . Woe to him who says to wood, 'Come to life!' . . . . .[For] there is no breath in it" (Hab. 2:18-19;NIV). It is only as the Spirit of God prompts us to dream again that we can cooperate with Him and see our dreams take the shape of His design.

Perhaps, even now as you read, the Holy Spirit is stirring in you. Something inside you is resonating. And the Spirit is gently prodding: "Prophesy to your monument of failure. Command your discarded dreams to take shape. Let them reconnect with the resurrected hopes of others. Dare to hope again!"

Do you hear the Spirit's command? Then let your response be the same as Ezekiel's: "So I prophesied as I was commanded" (Ezek. 37:7). Command your dry, dead dreams to take shape!

Flesh and Blood Dreams

In response to the prophet's command hopes began to take shape once again. Then the Spirit issued a second command to Ezekiel:

> Prophesy to the breath, prophesy, son of man, and say to the breath, Thus says the Lord God: Come from the four winds, O breath, and breathe on these slain, that they may live (Ezek. 37:9).

Ezekiel was to make a faith-filled appeal to God for the release of the Holy Spirit to animate the reconstructed hopes — this time actually to speak a command to *Him* to cause the newly shaped army to come to life. After he prophesied, "Breath came into them, and they lived and stood upon their feet" (Ezek. 37:10).

While many Christians are somewhat uncomfortable with the idea that we are told to "command" something from God, again it must be remembered that this is at God's prompting. In other passages God implores us to "ask of Me" (Ps. 2:8) and "prove Me" (Mal. 3:10).

God urges us to see how serious He is about the restoration of our dreams! He is actually saying, "Just ask Me to get involved once again in your hopes and dreams. You've been so discouraged you don't know if your secret longings can ever come back to life. But now is the time. Believe I can do what you cannot do. I want the privilege of breathing life back into your dreams."

Only God can make bones reconnect. And, certainly, only God can breathe life into them. But as we declare reverently, with faith, that God's Spirit will now breathe life into the shapes of our dreams, we are simply cooperating with the Holy Spirit as He develops what He has placed in our hearts.

I emphasize again that we are not at liberty to "think up" our own dream and then "confess" it into existence. However, not only are we at liberty to cooperate with Spirit-induced ideas, we are obliged to do so as obedient servants of Christ. Just as Mary pondered the angel's announcement in her heart, so your "sanctified pondering" helps your dreams. Let the Holy Spirit guide your thoughts and prayers. Allow Him to show you what your dream will look like when it is fully formed and mature.

Where the Credit Is Due

First, God commanded the prophet to speak to the bones. Second, He commanded him to speak to the wind.

A third and final time God commanded Ezekiel to prophesy. "Therefore prophesy and say to them, Thus says the Lord God: Behold, O My people, I will open your graves and . . . bring you into the land of Israel. Then you shall know that I am the Lord, when I have opened your graves, O my people, and brought you up from your graves. I will put My Spirit in you, and you shall live, and I will place you in your own land. Then you shall know that I, the Lord, have spoken it and performed it, says the Lord" (Ezek. 37:12-14).

Notice that the subject emblazoned on the revived people is "I, the Lord." "*I* will open your graves . . . ." "*I* will put My Spirit [My life] in you . . . ." "*I* will place you in your own land [a place of fulfillment] . . . ." "*I* have spoken it . . . ." "*I* have performed it . . . ." The people now have a new life and a new arena in which to live out their dreams. To whom do they owe such wonderful blessings? They can no longer even imagine that their dreams' fulfillment is the result of their own clever ideas. "*The Lord* has done great things for us, and we are glad" (Ps. 126:3).

Notice the analogy. First, Ezekiel was told to command his dreams to re-form. Second, he was told to implore the Spirit of God to breathe life into the renewed form of hope. Finally, the prophet was told to give total credit to the Lord. It was a miracle of God that turned the bones into a skeletal army. It was a miracle of God that breathed life into these newly formed corpses. And it was a miracle of God that would now strengthen this "exceedingly great army" of new hope to march to victory. No longer can the focus be on ourselves, but on the Creator, Recreator, Sustainer, and victorious Captain of our army of dreams. The Lord himself is the "author and finisher of our faith" (Heb. 12:2).

You now have renewed hopes. You also have a redirected point of reference. No longer is it your dream; it is His. Nor will the victory be yours when this dream, born first in His heart and then transplanted to yours, is fulfilled. The new hope within you, from inception to completion, is His.

Some years ago I was driving home from a weekend of ministry in a small town in central Texas. It was early spring. I rolled down the windows and inhaled the sweet, fresh air. The services had gone well and I was meditating on the goodness of God.

"Lord," I said, "thank You for working in my ministry today."

Immediately His loving correction came to my heart: *Whoever said it was yours?*

The dry bones, that monument to failure, can take form again. Your dreams can live again. How? By the word of the Lord. At His command, dead dreams stand up. By His breath they live again. Then, as Sovereign Lord of hopes and dreams, He declares, "I, the Lord, have done it."

13

A Fresh Cluster of Promise

Let us hold fast the confession of our hope without wavering, for He who promised is faithful (Heb. 10:23).

In 1980 I sat in the simple apartment of Dr. and Mrs. Paul Billheimer. "Mama" Billheimer had just taken the dishes from the table and Dr. Billheimer and I were reminiscing concerning the faithfulness of the Lord.

"A few years ago I thought my usefulness was finished," he told me. "Mama Billheimer and I had moved to a little cottage in the South. We bought cemetery lots and prepared to die. We were discouraged, defeated. Though we loved the Lord, we thought of the bitter mixture of our failures along with our few successes."

He paused. Tears welled up in his eyes. "Then God 'gave' me this little book." He picked up a nearby copy of *Destined for the Throne.* "Now I travel all over the world in ministry. Mama and I have a nationally televised program. I'm touching more people in a few weeks than I did in all my previous life of service. I call it my resurrection ministry."

This godly octogenarian had received a fresh cluster of promise. Like pebbles, the dreams that never came true seemed insignificant beside the pearl-like luster of the new dreams — dreams that once would have been beyond his fondest hopes.

As I sat and listened to that thrilling testimony, my heart was enraptured once again at the omniscient mercy of the Lord. How wonderfully like Jesus to "surprise" an eighty-plus-year-old person with unspeakable joy and fulfillment after so much heartache. "The Lord is good to all, and His tender mercies are over all His works" (Ps. 145:9).

The Cycles of Life

Few things in life are permanent — including success and failure. There are definite cycles in most of our lives. But there is one thing we can count on being constant, no matter what the circumstances. There is a way to experience solid living in unsettling times. That unchanging thing is the steadfast love of God. "I am the Lord, I do not change" (Mal. 3:6). "Through the Lord's mercies we are not consumed, because His compassions fail not. They are new every morning. Great is Your faithfulness. The Lord is my portion, says my soul, Therefore I hope in Him!" (Lam. 3:22-24).

With a bedrock confidence in God's faithfulness, we can weather the cycles of life. Paul said, "I have learned in whatever state I am, to be content" (Phil. 4:11). Life's cycles seem to go in something of a pattern. First, there is the God-birthed aspiration. Then, an attempt is made to realize the aspiration. After our hopes are frustrated, we take a few steps back and enter a period where we seem to be in a "holding pattern." During this time God works deeper character and integrity in us. Then, by His power, He speaks life back into our deflated hopes. Darkness gives way to light. Despair gives way to fresh hope. "Weeping may endure for a night, but joy comes in the morning" (Ps. 30:5).

No one is exempt from failure. But the measure of your life's accomplishments is not in the number of failures but in the tenacity of your spirit. The Bible says, "For a righteous man may fall seven times and rise again" (Prov. 24:16).

I've been told that Babe Ruth is the all-time strikeout king. That's an infamous distinction! But don't forget, until Hank Aaron, he was also the all-time home run king. Ruth was no rookie when it came to hitting. He could have "hedged." He would have struck out far fewer times if he had attempted more bunts or grounders past the infield. But Ruth wasn't shooting for singles; he was aiming for the nickel seats. So he was compelled to swing with all his might. And sometimes he looked pretty stupid when he missed the ball a country mile. But when he connected it was poetry in motion.

The point is, keep swinging! As you trust in the Lord, sooner or later you will "connect" and thousands will be affected. Again I remind you of what Vince Lombardi once said: "The greatest success is not in never failing but in rising every time you fall."

Have you fallen? Look around. You're far from alone. Your distinction is not in the fact that you have failed. Most, if not all, people do fail at some point. The distinction will be when you get back up — when you allow God to give you a fresh cluster of promise. Many people choose to stay down in the pile of broken humanity; you are created for better things. There's a future for you.

In our day perhaps the only kind of hero with whom people can really identify is a tarnished hero. Politicians, preachers, educators, doctors — every profession that has been revered historically — has been soiled by highly publicized scandals. In all the distorted noise of the last few years there is perhaps only one clear message that's gotten through, one statement with which all of us, Christian and secular alike, would agree: Nobody's perfect.

From now on it may well be that we will have a new

definition of the word *hero*. In the past, we thought of a hero as one who was free from even the hint of embarrassing incrimination. But in today's world, and by the new definition forced on us by life's hard realities, the real heroes are the drug addicts who break free, the teenagers who live responsibly in the face of their parents' alcoholism, the prostitutes who become Christian ladies, and the broken, repentant, and rehabilitated preachers who humbly and gratefully speak once again in His name.

So get up. Nothing lasts forever — except the mercy of God.

For the unbeliever the cycles of life end on the downside. But for the Christian, life's cycles end on the upswing. This is not your last taste of trouble. Nor is it your last taste of victory in spite of trouble. Christ's overcoming power will be just as potent the next time around as it is in this present moment. "In the world you will have tribulation; but be of good cheer, I have overcome the world" (John 16:33).

In the early 1980s, I faced a time of acute discouragement while battling the temptation to throw in the towel. At that strategic moment, God brought a seasoned pastor across my path — literally. He knew nothing of my present despondency. In fact, we had only a brief meeting on a sidewalk. After an exchange of greetings, he said, "David, just don't give up. It's always too soon to quit. No matter what the problems, don't stop. Just don't give up!" Then he walked away.

What that pastor did not know was that he was a God-sent prophet that day to a young preacher on the edge. As Bob Pierce once said, "The secret to lasting success is *lasting*."

It is not of ultimate consequence that you have fallen down. What ultimately matters is that you are standing up when the dust settles. A weak second quarter will indeed set you back, but it's the final quarter that makes the real difference. You will win if you will get up. The only way you will lose is if you forfeit the game.

During another especially stressful "cycle" of my life, while I was in seminary, I remember literally pacing the floor of our little bedroom. "Naomi," I blurted, "it's like God has forgotten our address. I have no sense of His presence. He's not treating me like a son!"

Immediately my heart rebuked me. Lovingly, the Lord reminded me, *That's exactly the way I am treating you.*

Are you being pressed — even by the Lord? As a father prods his son to noble accomplishments, so your Father is pressing you toward greater heights. His dealings with you are not indiscriminate. They are well-designed discipline, ordained to produce results. Don't forget it, as others have done: "And you have forgotten the exhortation which speaks to you as to sons: 'My son, do not despise the chastening of the Lord, nor be discouraged when you are rebuked by Him; for whom the Lord loves He chastens, And scourges every son whom He receives.' If you endure chastening, God deals with you as with sons" (Heb. 12:5-7).

Don't become even more fatigued by trying to figure out the reason for the chastening. Simply endure the chastening as a child in whom the Father delights. The believer who understands the purpose of pressure can relax in the wisdom of God, knowing that He does all things well. "My brethren, count it all joy when you fall into various trials, knowing that the testing of your faith produces patience. But let patience have its perfect work, that you may be perfect and complete, lacking nothing" (James 1:2-4). What better qualification could there be for future blessings than to be "perfect and complete, lacking nothing!"

The cycles of life continue to swing back and forth like a pendulum or ebb and flow like the tide. And the downswings of the cycles are purposeful; they produce a thrill and exhilaration when the cycle (as it inevitably will) swings up again.

"I Will Restore"

As I'm sure you know by now, I believe very much in the sovereign workings of God. For the Christian, there are no chance encounters. God loves you. His highest joy is that the purpose of your life be fulfilled. He is offering you a fresh cluster of promise — luminescent pearls in the place of worn pebbles.

There are three specific items God extends to you in this fresh cluster of promise. First, he wants to *renew your mind*. He wants to give you the capacity to think clearly again. He wants to free you from morbidity, pessimism, and despair. He wants to empower you to stay level when others are imbalanced. The challenges of our times demand gargantuan thinkers — God-inspired dreamers who can see past the problems to heaven's answer.

God has an answer for society-threatening epidemics. God has an answer to the inequities caused by avarice and greed. God has an answer to the aggression of ungodly nations. God has an answer to fractured marriages and rebellious children. He has an answer for your agony. He's looking for those who qualify to be entrusted with heaven's answers.

Will you receive His offer of a renewed mind? Then turn to Him and ask Him to purify your heart and mind. "For the eyes of the Lord run to and fro throughout the whole earth, to show himself strong on behalf of those whose heart is loyal to Him" (2 Chron. 16:9).

God also is ready to *rekindle your dream*. Fresh fire is being lit even now in your heart. You're ready to start over. All that you presently see began as a dream, a dream from God. "Every good gift and every perfect gift is from above, and comes down from the Father of lights, with whom there is no variation or shadow of turning" (James 1:17). Though it will be in a new form, your dream will be recognizable; it will be similar and yet beautifully different from the one you first cherished long ago. The time wasn't right then. And maybe the dream wasn't exactly right. But it's time to begin again. God offers you re-kindled dreams.

And three, God's fresh cluster of promise includes a wonderful surprise: You haven't lost any time! The Lord is willing to *restore the years*. God promised that the outpouring of His Spirit would signal a new era of restoration. And, without question, God's Spirit is being poured out in unprecedented fashion around the world. This can only mean that you too can be included. "And let him who thirsts come. Whoever desires, let him take the water of life freely" (Rev. 22:17).

The thief has come to destroy. But Christ has come to restore all that has been temporarily lost. What has taken the devil years to unravel slowly, Jesus Christ can restore instantly.

God gave Joel a sneak preview of this epoch of the Spirit's outpouring. Lives would be restored. Nations would be restored. Spiritual gifts would be restored. And, perhaps most amazingly, time itself would be restored. "So I will restore to you the years that the swarming locust has eaten" (Joel 2:25). The "locusts" of failure, hurt, and bitterness may have eaten away at your very life, consuming your most precious commodity: time. But now, through the unspeakable mercy of God, He will restore even the years to you that the locusts have eaten.

> *The "locusts" of failure, hurt, and bitterness may have eaten away at your very life, consuming your most precious commodity: time. But now, through the unspeakable mercy of God, He will restore even the years to you that the locusts have eaten.*

God will compact your life with effectiveness, allowing you to accomplish in months what used to take years, and enabling you to accomplish in days what might otherwise have taken a lifetime. "For with God *nothing* will be impossible" (Luke 1:37).

On High Places

Your midnight is over. God is giving you a fresh cluster of promise: a renewed mind, rekindled dreams, and restored years. Even now hopes are being reshaped in the white-hot smeltery of His love. As you refocus on Jesus himself, and as your hopes are refined and, yes, redefined by Him, a wonderful side effect occurs. Your heart is no longer enraptured with dreams and personal ambitions. Jesus Christ is your heart's delight. Then, once again, His irrepressible love for you breaks through. Your heart's delight is the Lord Jesus. But He gives you your other orbiting desires — your dreams — as well. "Delight yourself also in the Lord, and He shall give you the desires of your heart" (Ps. 37:4).

You've traveled in the valley of mourning long enough. Your next stop is with princes: "He raises the poor out of the dust, and lifts the needy out of the ash heap, that He may seat him with princes — with the princes of His people" (Ps. 113:7-8).

Like the prophet Habakkuk, you are destined to walk the high places of the earth. Habakkuk had faced his unrealized dreams head on. He had made allowances for past disappointments. But his faith in God's future for him burned brighter than ever. He had closed the book on past unrealized hopes. Now he turned with a joyful heart to the high experiences just ahead — and to the God who would lead him there.

"The Lord God is my strength; He will make my feet like deer's feet, and He will make me walk on my high hills" (Hab. 3:19). Get ready. Your new adventure is about to begin.

Notes

Chapter One

1. William Shakespeare, *The Tempest IV*, i, p. 156.
2. Winston Churchill, Tribute to Neville Chamberlain, House of Commons, November 12, 1940.
3. Alexander Pope, *An Essay on Man*, Epistle I, p. 95.
4. Ella Wheeler Wilcox, "The Winds of Fate," *The Best Loved Poems of the American People*, compiled by Hazel Felleman (Garden City, NY: Doubleday & Co., 1936) p. 364, 1st stanza.

Chapter Three

1. Matthew Arnold, *Thyrsis*, Stanza 14, (1866).

Chapter Five

1. Ian Thomas, *The Saving Life of Christ* (Grand Rapids, MI: Zondervan Publishing House, 1961).
2. V. Raymond Edman, *They Found the Secret* (Grand Rapids, MI: Zondervan Publishing House, 1960).
3. John Pollock, *Billy Graham* (Grand Rapids, MI: Zondervan Publishing House, 1966), p. 19.
4. Elisabeth Elliot, *Through Gates of Splendor* (Wheaton, IL: Tyndale House, Publishers, 1981).

Chapter Seven

1. William Butler Yeats, *He Wishes for the Cloths of Heaven* (1899).
2. Elizabeth Skoglund, *Coping* (Glendale, CA: Regal Books, 1979), p. 44-45.
3. Used by permission of Evangelical Publishers, a division of Scripture Press Publications, Ltd.

Chapter Nine

1. John Rippon, *A Selection of Hymns from the Best Authors* (1787).

Chapter Ten

1. Paul E. Billheimer, *Don't Waste Your Sorrows* (Fort Washington, PA: Christian Literature Crusade, 1977) p. 79-80.

Chapter Eleven

1. Copyright © 1974 by Jensen Music/ASCAP. Used by permission of the Benson Co., Inc., Nashville, TN.
2. Fanny J. Crosby, *Rescue the Perishing* (1869).

David Shibley

David Shibley is president and founder of Global Advance, a missions ministry equipping and resourcing national church leaders to reach their own people and surrounding peoples with the gospel. With over a quarter century of fruitful ministry, he has ministered in over thirty nations. Also, he travels extensively throughout the United States, speaking in behalf of world evangelization.

Mr. Shibley knows what works from a lifetime of missions involvement. A clear vision has emerged in his heart to quickly, sensitively, and cost-effectively fulfill Christ's Great Commission. The key lies with national church leaders — frontline shepherds. Global Advance equips these leaders for world harvest through Frontline Shepherds Conferences in many nations. These strategic leaders leave with a vision in their hearts and tools in their hands.

In addition to his ministry with Global Advance, Mr. Shibley serves on eight missions boards and is a member of the far-reaching U.S. Lausanne Committee on World Evangelization. He is the author of eight books and numerous articles.

A graduate of John Brown University in Arkansas, and Southwestern Baptist Theological Seminary, he holds an honorary doctorate from ORU. He and his wife, Naomi, have two sons.

For more information regarding the ministry of Global Advance and David Shibley, contact:

Global Advance
P.O. Box 222
Rockwall, TX 75087-0222

(214) 771-9042
FAX (214) 722-6119